Growing Up in Communist Albania

NOSH MERNACAJ

ISBN: 9798723624207

To my family who sacrificed so much under communist oppression.

To all Albanian people who lived under the communist regime.

To all people around the globe who continue to suffer under oppressive dictatorships.

Contents

I want to thank everyone who encouraged me to take on this project. Thank you to all who helped me with it: Monika Koleci, Professor. Frederick Akamine (RIP), and Rebecca Goldberg.
Special thanks to my editor, Barry Lyons.

Thank you to all the readers who are taking a chance on my first book.

Growing Up in
Communist Albania

1. Never Forget

"The North Korean dictator is dead!" I heard my fiancée shout this from behind the glass doors that led to the living area of my hotel room. With my eyes half-opened, a pillow covering my face, and in a semi-awake mode, I wasn't sure I heard her correctly, but I wished my ears were not deceiving me.

It was around ten o'clock in the morning of December 17, 2011, at my ocean view suite of Eden Rock Renaissance Resort in Miami Beach, Florida. Because of my frequent traveler status, I had been upgraded to the nicest suite with a large ocean view balcony, a Jacuzzi, a floor-to-ceiling glass living area, a large flat-screen television, and modern furnishing all around. This was an unparalleled luxury for most of us today and for sure it was something I had never even dreamed of while growing up.

My fiancée was awake before me and was watching the news in the living room. I like watching news but tend not to on my vacation. However, I couldn't miss this news item. First thing I did that day when I woke up was to go to the balcony. The ocean breeze filled my lungs. A majestic view lay ahead of me. The sun was gold and warm, warm enough for December in Florida and for sure much warmer than in New York, where I live. The water was calm. A merchant vessel broke the line of the horizon here and there, but otherwise the ocean's end could be drawn with such precision as if it were on a small paper. A Jet Ski or sailboat went past here and there. Some seagulls were looking to steal a breakfast from a bystander. Somewhere on the beach a mother was running after her kid who couldn't get his kite fly right. A couple was walking holding hands. The hotel staff were doing their morning chores. Some guests were returning from breakfast. Some guests were heading for the ocean. Others were standing by the pool. People were having a good time. Marvelous. Just wonderful. God-made beauty combined with man-made resorts and hotels lining beside a silhouette of palm trees and white sand. We had come here to celebrate my thirty-third birthday. Life is great, I thought. I came back inside and jumped back on the bed after admiring the view of the Miami coastline and thanking God for the opportunities it had granted me.

"The North Korean dictator is dead!" She had said for a second time or third until I acknowledged her. Maybe she said "President of North Korea," or something along those lines, I can't remember, but who really cares what his official title is or what my fiancée called him. All dictators like to be called by some grand royal names, and some of them give themselves so many titles that when addressing them you need to take pauses so as not to run out of breath while going through the long list. What really mattered was that the devil was dead.

"Really?" "When?" "How?" I bombarded her with questions, not believing the news.

After she explained the details to me and ascertained the fact by seeing what was on television, I sat down. The large screen seemed so small now and I wanted to enter inside it to feel it.

"This is the best birthday gift I've received in a very long time," I said.

Kim Jong-Ill, dictator of North Korea, the oppressor of its own people, the devil incarnate, had in fact died. Why would that make me, one would ask, so happy? North Korea is far away. I don't know anyone there. I have never visited the country. I have no connection to this country whatsoever, yet the death of its dictator gave me so much joy! When Enver Hoxha, the communist dictator of Albania—the country I grew up in—died, I was seven years old and unable to fully understand. Ramiz Alia, the next in line, took over and nothing changed for the people. We couldn't celebrate but had to mourn or the communist regime would punish anyone who dared not to mourn the death of the "Albanian Savior," as he liked to be called, pulling a title from one of his long lists of titles. There were many diehard communists, sympathizers, supporters, and some brainwashed individuals who really mourned his death, but for the masses this was a celebration: too bad it was one that couldn't be acknowledged out loud. The regime would beat, torture, imprison, and even execute anyone who dared not to mourn. I couldn't ever imagine my parents shedding any tears for that monster. Now I'm a grown-up man and live in a country of immense freedom, but I cannot forget my past: a past that looks a lot like the pictures of North Korea of today streaming from television screens. We see, yet do not believe, nor care maybe, and continue our blessed lives, enjoying the freedoms we take for granted. It is, thus, very close to heart for me. I feel the death of this dictator as if it were the death of Enver Hoxha, the dictator who shaped my life until the age of fourteen. I could tell it was going to be a very good day.

I was born in a small town called Mali i Jushit in the district of Shkodër in northern Albania in 1976. The communist regime was at its peak and with no signs of weakening anytime soon. My family was one from a class of people called "Të Prekun." The direct translation to English is "the touched," which has a connotation similar to "the possessed," as in being controlled by daemons. This was a label used to identify people who dared stand up to the regime in any way or anyone who fell out of favor with communist rule. People from this so-called class were called many names, from Të Prekun to Armiq të Popullit ("enemy of the people"). The list went on and on. Të Prekun was the official title of the class, but there was another bizarre name used, Të Deklasuem, which means "declassed," as someone who does not belong to any class. It meant we were not even worth living. Without any remorse nor shame, whenever we requested anything, such as permission to buy a bicycle, the answer was, "We can't. You know you are Të Deklasuem, or Të Prekun."

So where did we belong then? My parents didn't dream of me going to college nor having anything other than a small house near theirs, perhaps, and marry a girl they would pick for me, have lots of kids and work in the Kooperativë, which was the name given to the collective farming enterprise owned and operated by the government. A Kooperativë (collective farming) was the goal: to make the communist regime the only landowner in the country. A Kooperativë comprised one or many small villages, depending on the size of the village, and all residents from the age of fourteen, unless they went to high school, were required to register and become part of the workforce. All land and livestock were sequestered from every citizen and became government property. From that point on, any possession of private property was strictly forbidden. Why reinvent the wheel, when the Soviets have already done so? Not to mention that most of the methods established in Albania came straight from Russian playbook of Joseph Stalin. Albanian communists just took it even further. Stalin would envy them. The word "Kooperativë" was not only used to define the economic structure of collective farming, it was also used in some cases as a synonym to define a municipality or an area where the Kooperativë was situated. Kooperativë usually comprised one or more small towns, or one municipality, so the words "town" and "Kooperativë" were used interchangeably. It was common, thus, for people to say, "I live in the Kooperativë of Barbullush" instead of "I live in the town of Barbullush." My future, just like most of my parents' past, was written in simple sentences, and was to be anything but bright. Fate had it that the communist regime collapsed in 1992 and I live in one of the most democratic countries on the face of earth, but events like these bring me right back to where I was born and spent the worst days of my life: days that should have been the best.

2. Family History

My family's origins can be traced back ten generations. That is how far anyone alive has any recollection of it. As far as any documented history, we have none. Most foreign occupying countries that ruled Albania for centuries were not really concerned with preserving the past, and the communists simply burned down everything to start new. Given the lack of any documents, pictures, paintings, or anything tangible, it is pretty impressive to even be able to trace the roots that far.

We trace the origins to a small village in the highlands called Selcë, in the Kelmend area. To this day, we identify among people with knowledge of the area as Seljan, a person from Selcë, or Kelmend, a person from the greater Kelmend region. Kelmend is located in the most northern point of Albania that borders with Montenegro.[1] Like the rest of the people from the same region, my ancestors were mostly shepherds who spent half the year, the warm months of the year, in the highlands of Kelmend mountains—or what could be called their permanent home, and when it got colder and snow covered all their homes,

---

[1] Depending on the historical period, Montenegro has existed as a sovereign nation/country and at some other times has been part of the Yugoslavian Federation, aka Yugoslavia. We will use the names Montenegro and Yugoslavia according to the times the events took place. During the period when Montenegro was part of the Yugoslavian Federation, it was one of the six republics that made up the Federation: Slovenia, Croatia, Serbia, Bosnia and Herzegovina, Montenegro, and Macedonia. Today, they are all independent countries.

too cold for people and livestock, they went down the mountains into warmer areas where they could find green pastures for their animals and bearable temperatures for themselves. They had to pay a small tariff for using the valleys for grazing in these areas, but that tariff wasn't high and well worth it. At some point, they decided to settle in the warm region near Adriatic Sea and started building more permanent homes and later bought land in the flatlands in the regions of lower Shkodër and Lezhë. This region starts at the river of Buna, in the north and extends all the way to Durrës in the south. This is the Adriatic coastline with many swamps and valleys that made it suitable for people who only knew how to raise animals. They continued the same arrangement for many more years, but the permanent home became the lower Shkodër and not the Alps. According to some historians, most notably Friar Zef Pllumi[2] in his memoir *"Histori Kurrë e Shkrueme"* —A Story Never Written Before, the permanent migration from the Alps to the lower Shkodër area happened around 1750s when Mehmet Bushatliu was the Ottoman Turkish governor of Shkodër. He gave the lands to these highlanders to reward them for their help in the wars against his rivals. I will contend that it happened, because I

---

[2] Friar Zef Pllumi is also from the same region and has had access to documents that were housed at the Franciscan seminary in Shkodër where he studied. Those documents were burned by the Communist regime and their witnesses are all dead. Due to lack of any documentation on my possession, I cannot attest to this claim. I can only accept it as a plausible option. This is a topic of further study and out of scope for the purposes of this book.

definitely don't like mountains and cold. After a long period of time, some managed to buy small parcels of lands and build homes. The land was fertile and the weather was warm. Farming, unknown to them before, became a new way of life. The house I grew up in, was the very first house built in the whole town of Mali i Jushit, a town founded and populated exclusively from these highlanders.

Albania had been under the rule of the Ottoman Empire for about 500 years until 1912 when it became independent, thanks in large part to the United States and the continuous support of Woodrow Wilson in particular. In and around 1910, the Ottoman army was conducting a campaign against the Christian population of the area. The Ottoman Empire was an Islamic empire and these highlanders were predominantly Christian. For centuries they had converted a large part of the Albanian population to Islam. My family never converted from Christianity to Islam and that was something they were proud of. Frightened villagers gathered what they could and left their homes to go into hiding. A majority of the population had already been converted into Islam by then, and the Ottoman Turks[3] wanted to get hold of the rest of the population—the

---

[3] Modern day Turkey was established on the ruins of Ottoman Empire; Turkey is the de facto direct descendent of the Ottoman Empire. *Ottomans* and *Turks* may be used as synonyms in many respects when referencing the governing body of the empire, even though many countries occupied by the Ottoman Empire contributed and served in the Ottoman Empire as well.

stubborn minority of Christians—and convert them all at any cost. The Ottoman Empire was already collapsing in many parts in the east and the west and so these were desperate moves by the Turks to keep control. Large armies marched into small and big towns burning and destroying everything in their path.

Zef was a little boy, only five years of age, and somehow got separated from his parents. He was found in Ulqin,[4] Montenegro, a town about ten kilometers away, but died shortly after from an unknown disease. Zef was my uncle, the first-born child of my grandparents Marash Gjeka and Maruke Gjergj-ja. Later, my own father was also named Zef, in memory of my uncle, the young victim of Ottoman brutality. After Zef, my grandparents had six more children: one girl and five boys. They were Nocë, Nikë, Gjon, Gjekë, Kolë, and my father Zef. In 1932, when my father was only four years old, his father died from one of the common diseases of the time due to the lack of any medical attention. It was called common because many people died of unknown causes due to lack of medical attention, but no one knew the cause of death. He was about forty-five years old. No one knew for sure the real age due to lack of any reliable birth certificates or records. In fact, most ages presented here, besides my generation, are approximations.

---

[4] Since this is an Albanian city that was taken by Montenegro, I will call it by its Albanian name, Ulqin. In the language of Montenegro, it is spelled Ulcinj.

My grandmother raised six kids by herself. Struggles never went away, but somehow she made it. As the older kids grew up, some—Nocë, Nikë, and Gjon— got married and started their own families. The family tree started to blossom and expand again. Mother was getting older and the kids were maturing. Better times started to appear on the horizon. One country after the other occupied Albania, from Italy to Germany, and boys were called to serve in the army, mostly the occupying Italian army. All of them came home safe and went back to their normal lives. Now all the boys were able to work. Finally, the family was able to buy a piece of land adjacent to theirs and grow more crops and raise more livestock. That will be short-lived though, because the communists would soon take over everything shortly after.

I. A Delusional Victory

"*Mos u gzo i gzuem, mos u idhno i idhnuem,*" says one of my favorite Albanian proverbs. No matter how many times I think of this line it sounds truer more and more every time. It loosely translates into: "If you are happy, don't be joyful; if you are sad, don't be gloomy." The moral of this proverb is that when you feel that you have nothing else to lose, something good will come, whereas if you feel all is good, something bad will come. Or you can say it can also mean don't take anything for granted, good or bad. Life is full of great surprises and disappointments.

While most of the world was celebrating the end of World War II, especially war-torn Europe, Albania was entering one of the darkest chapters of its history—a looming communist dictatorship—even though they didn't know yet. Catholic clergy had been preaching about the dangers of Bolsheviks and communists for years, but the majority of the population was ignorant and didn't appreciate this warning. As my uncle Gjon would say, "All those words went in one ear and out the other." The last German soldier left Albania on November 29, 1944, the date recognized as the liberation of Albania from Nazi/fascist occupation: essentially the end of World War II for Albania. World War II was a bloody war and left many scars around the world. In the middle of it all, Albania was not immune.

Albanians had joined the fight in any way they could, whether it was directly joining the guerrillas or helping with logistics and other tasks required to carry on a resistance; Albanians did not stay idle. There were several Albanian guerrillas, but three of them were the dominating forces: Partisan, Ballist, and Legalist. All of them were fighting for the liberation of Albania, but each had a different idea of what to do with it after the war. These three factions were very much adversaries. Albania had been a parliamentary monarchy before the Italian occupation. Even though attempts were made to create a unified front regardless of party affiliation for the good of the country and to be more efficient, those attempts failed because partisans had other plans for them. Partisans were the forces lead by the Communist Party. Ballists were the guerrillas lead by the "Balli Kombetar" Party. The Legalists were the guerrillas made of the exiled King Zog's party members and supporters. They were also known as Zogists (supporters of King Zog). This group had a lot of ex-military officers and soldiers of the old Albanian army, since King Zog was the last Albanian leader before Italy invaded Albania in 1939. Legalists were the best-trained armed forces then. Most of their officers had studied in some of the best schools of Europe and Turkey. These parties did not see eye to eye, and as the end of the war was nearing, the communists started to consolidate the power by going after Ballist and Legalist members.

Communist persecution started even before the end of the war and continued after the war until they had been declared the sole power to take Albania into the after-war journey. In fact, communists fought a war against Albanian adversaries more than a war against Fascist Italians or Nazi Germans who were too powerful even for the greatest armies of the world.

Yugoslavia has been the historical foe of Albania.[5] Many times in its history, Serbia and Montenegro have attacked Albanian lands and even succeeding in taking over parts of it for periods of time. The creation of a Yugoslavian federation where the dominating republic was Serbia, a unified Yugoslavia was seen as the continuation of Serbia and Montenegro. They have never ceased their wish to one day take over the entire country of Albania. In times of war, Albanian clans and tribes rallied together against the old enemy and succeeded in keeping large armies of Serbia and Montenegro ashore. Wars were fought during the Ottoman Empire as well between Ottomans defending Albania under the Empire and Serbo-Montenegrins trying to rip pieces from it. It was like a bunch of hyenas looking to steal a lion's lunch. Yugoslavia had already taken over good parts of northern Albania as part of the Berlin treaty of 1878, which gave those lands to Montenegro, but Albania was still

---

[5] The enemies in question have been only the two republics of Yugoslavia; Serbia and Montenegro. The rest of the republics that made up Yugoslavia now, Slovenia, Croatia, Bosnia and Herzegovina, and Macedonia, were not part of those conflicts.

standing on its feet despite being truncated by all sides. Since the Albanian fortress was too strong to take over from outside, maybe Yugoslavs could try to take it from within. What a better way than to use one of the oldest tricks in the world: deception. Either the Albanian communists were too naïve, or the Yugoslav Machiavellian communists were too clever, or both, but somehow these two groups had become brothers united to fight the Albanian patriots who had always been at war with Serbia and Montenegro to protect their lands. Now, without firing a shot, the Yugoslavs were welcomed with open arms to do with Albania as they pleased. No one would have ever imagined such a day would arrive. I am sure the Yugoslavs must have laughed at the ignorance of these Albanian morons who allowed them entry into their land Yugoslavs had always wished to have theirs, or better, begged them to come in. The Communist Party of Albania was formed in 1941 with the direction and support of Yugoslav communists.

At the end of the war, having weakened or eliminated all competition, the Communist Party of Albania, led by Enver Hoxha, was the de facto only force to lead Albania. As the new communist provisional government was trying to establish an army on its own, my father, who was only sixteen at the time, was called to serve in the military. My uncle Gjekë was already discharged. The other three brothers had served in the Italian army, and so they were exempt. Even though the communists had already taken control of the country after its liberation in November 29, 1944, the fate of Albania would be permanently sealed at the conference of Potsdam, Germany in July/August of 1945.[6] Albania, thus, was given to Russia as a war prize to do with it as it pleased, together with the rest of Eastern Europe. The Red Army of the Soviet Union[7] was a deciding force in the war against Hitler, so it was decided to replace one monster with another in half of Europe, Hitler with Stalin. The Western world had been liberated while the East had been betrayed. Albania has had one of the worst communist regimes in the world, maybe the worst by many standards. Time and time again in history, Albanians had been treated as property to be traded for favors among great powers of the world. This time was no different. The communist regime came to power as part of the deal between the winners of the World War II: the United States, the Soviet Union and their allies, so there was little or nothing any Albanian could do about it but to embrace it. Even so, many people did stand up and fought and failed. They were just too weak to fight the communist devil with Russian backing.

---

[6] The conference of Potsdam was held between the allies to decide the future of liberated countries. Albania was given to Russia to decide its political affiliation. To no one's surprise, it was Communism.

[7] The USSR, also known as the Soviet Union, was the country comprising 17 countries united under one flag. Russia was the main power, thus Russia—USSR—Soviet Union are used as synonyms. They do mean slightly different things today.

Albania is a very small country in the Balkan Peninsula with about four million people today.[8] There are another three million people outside the political borders of Albania in Albanian lands that were taken away by one treaty or another[9]. For the purposes of this book and for the benefit of the Western reader and people unfamiliar with the geography and geopolitics of the region, we will refer to Albania as the Republic of Albania and not the Greater Albanian Region consisting of Kosovo, parts of Montenegro, parts of Northern Macedonia, and parts of Greece, all of whom identify as Albanian and live on autochthon Albanian lands. Furthermore, those parts of greater Albania weren't part of the atrocities I am bringing to the reader. They had their own struggles, but that is not the scope of this book. Little did we know, at least for the majority of the people, about the decisions made on behalf of our country by the great powers. The ones who did, the educated class, was quickly purged and eliminated. We didn't know there was a treaty that decided our fate growing up. Instead, we blamed this or that person, group, party, or country, even God. How could we know? The only information available was the highly censured, politicized, and crafted by the communist regime. We knew, what they wanted

---

[8] Today refers to year 2021.

[9] Albanian lands have been given to neighboring countries from different treaties in history as big powers decided to gift to their friends and allies. Most recent one was the Berlin treaty that gave large parts of northern Albania to Montenegro: Hot, Grude, Plave, Gusi, and Ulqin.

18

us to know and how they wanted us to know it. We were told lies for such a long time that eventually we may have begun to believe them after some time. We were free from Germans but not free at all because soon we became the slaves of Communism. As the Albanian proverb says, "nga shiu, ne breshër," which means "from rain to hail." So much for freedom.

The communists consolidated power and eliminated anyone who opposed them and those they feared might oppose them: preemptive striking. Most notably, intellectuals and anyone with little education were imprisoned and/or killed without any reason or due process. Public executions were commonplace for many years after World War II, with the justification of eliminating domestic enemies who supposedly had aided the foreign occupiers. A firing squad usually did the job of judge, jury, and executioner. Besides the partisan brigades that operated for many years as in wartime, there were certain individuals appointed and vested with all the power to execute anyone at will without any due process whatsoever. These people possessed a so-called carte blanche (ironically, there's no word in Albanian for carte blanche) that gave them absolute power over a territory. They rode on motorcycles left behind from Italians and Germans and even wore some parts of their old uniforms from town to town to cleanse them from anti-communists and spread terror. After killing someone, they would write their names into the list. Cart blanche, thus, was an empty list that had to be filled with the names of those who were eliminated. Sounds like a modern highly paid hit man job except that the target is chosen by the hit man himself. When these individuals were spotted speeding their motorcycles into a town, people ran away like zebras at the sight of a lion. People were killed for the simple crime of having pursued some education. These people were dangerous to the system because they had a better understanding of the situation and would have become a threat. Once the country was clean—and by clean I mean without an educated class—it was now time for another class to be created, a class that resembled a robotic program build by the CIA[10] and programmed to do exactly what they wanted and how they wanted it. Nothing more and nothing less. A class completely brainwashed. Loyal to no one but the Communist Party.

In the beginning, Albanians were excited to have an Albanian government after so many years of occupation from any country who set eyes on Albania, from the Ancient Roman Empire to 500 years of medieval Turkish Ottoman rule to the short but bloody German Nazi rule. With the exception of some short-lived Albanian governments between 1912 and 1939,

---

[10] Central Intelligence Agency—the spy agency in the United States—is widely known as the CIA.

Albania had been ruled by foreign rulers for most of its history. Thus, the idea of being governed by a government of the people, by the people, and for the people, resonated with the masses. Seems natural, but these dreams started to fade away very shortly after and Albanians had to brace for a very big surprise. The country fell into the harshest communist regime known to mankind. Persecutions started to spare no one: from high-level Party members to simple workers. People who had given everything they had to liberate their country from Nazis were now the enemy of the Communist Party, or the "enemy of the people" as the communists labeled them. Anyone who disagreed with the Party or expressed any discontent whatsoever was persecuted. No one was spared. No one.

My father and his family had been excited as well of the new deal. At merely sixteen, he wore the military uniform with the communist star in his beret and proudly called himself partisan. Partisans were freedom guerrilla fighters, and after the war, communists raged a hidden war to consolidate power and to ensure that no one would oppose them. Partisans (who weren't called soldiers) didn't need a mandate to kill as long as someone was suspected of any wrongdoing. Of course, most partisan units were honest patriots with the sole purpose of liberating and defending their country, but communists with their hidden agenda had infiltrated and then took over.

II.   In the Beginning

While my father, full of youthful optimism, was proudly serving his country, his older brothers had gotten in trouble with the government. The once very vocal freedom supporters of a promising Albanian government everyone longed to see installed were now the sworn enemies of the government once the government came to power. Like many people, they had soon realized the new government was a wolf in sheep's clothing. They didn't agree with almost anything that was happening, especially the confiscation of property and collectivization of the lands. Albania had been in a semi-feudal system for a long time before the war where most of the lands in the south were owned by landlords mainly appointed by the old Turkish Ottoman system. In the north it was a little different. Most northerners were owners of their own lands, small parcels as they may have been. The communists didn't make a difference, but treated them all the same. A reform, called the Agrarian Reform, took place in 1946, where all the farmland was confiscated by the government and equally distributed among all people living in those towns. That was just the first step into nationalizing all lands. Kooperativë was next. It happened sooner than anyone thought, when the town of Barbullush became the first Kooperativë in the country. This was advertised as being voluntary, but by communist standards there was nothing that you could refuse. At this point, no one owned any land beyond the perimeter around the house, which was limited to a 1000 square meters. My uncles could not sit idle to this grave injustice and worked hard to convince people to resist. They succeeded in dismantling the first fragile Kooperativë. This upset the regime. My uncles became a target and the local government did all they could to get them out of the way, literally.

Our house was built of raw stones. The walls were painted white throughout. Seemed the original walls had some decorations, as you could see here and there where the paint had peeled off, but now no one could afford to restore the original paint. Every once in a while, we would make a project to paint the walls, always white with chalkstone, because that was all we could get. Chalkstone is not a real paint, but when the chockstone is melted and becomes mud, it is then thinned to a point it makes this matter that looks like paint. It does the job. They say it is also a good sanitary product. Windows were small with some old curtains, which besides offering little privacy covered the rotten wooden frames. The walls were very plain with no decorations or pictures on them, besides the Lahuta (lute), an old Albanian folk instrument built by hand by my uncle Gjekë out of boredom when he was a young shepherd boy. My father played the Lahuta a lot, sometimes for entertainment and sometimes because it reminded him of his brothers. The only other item on those walls was a portrait of my father.

The photograph, above, was very old worn out from age and humidity. It was a black and white portrait. In that photograph, he was young and handsome and looked stoic. For most of my childhood it never occurred to me, but at some point in the later years when I examined the photo closely, it struck me that he was wearing a military uniform. Yet he didn't look 20 (the age he had been discharged). He looked much older. I had always thought that the picture was taken sometime during his time in the military. Instead, the photo was taken after his release from prison, which was long after his military discharge, internment camp, and prison time. In total, it was about fifteen years later. I asked him if he was wearing it because he was proud of the contribution he had made for the country, but I was mistaken. Yes, he was proud of serving his country but was now disappointed about what came next and, no, he would not have kept the uniform had he had a choice. He said that after his military discharge he was taken straight to an internment camp, then to prison, so he had no other clothes. Those were the best clothes he possessed and the picture was taken several months after his wedding in 1962. The black ribbon on the jacket is a tradition that means the person is in mourning for a loved one. Uncle Nikë had died that year. Women wore black scarves, and all their clothes were dark—or possibly black for mourning.

The regime was set in motion after the dissolution of the first Kooperativë where my uncles played a vital role and my uncle Kolë was arrested in the winter of 1947 under some fake accusations. An old woman in our town who lived by herself had been brutally murdered, and my uncles Kolë and Gjekë were accused of her murder.

III.   A Heinous Crime

The dictatorship of Enver Hoxha didn't need an excuse to arrest and persecute anyone. They did it all the time. People were executed publicly without due process all over the country. Nua Gjetja for instance, a distant relative of ours, was executed at a town meeting because he was tasked to confiscate all weapons, and at the meeting was asked if there were any illegal weapons in town. He replied, "no." Two days after his death, he was declared not guilty. He was the town mayor, but someone didn't like that he was popular among people and communists could not be friends with commoners. So why then go to such a great length to commit murder to frame my uncles? There is one explanation only: this was an attempt to turn the whole town against my family who otherwise enjoyed popularity. It was a strategic move. If my uncles were to be arrested for anything except for something like murder, which everyone condemns, their support would have just grown stronger. For a short time, my uncle was a local hero who stood up to the regime. No one in their right mind would support a murderer. Furthermore, these tactics were meant to terrorize and "teach a lesson" to others who may dare.

Dilë Gjekja, as she was known, was an old woman of about seventy years of age who never married. She lived by herself in a small house next to her relatives. My family is distantly related to her as well. You could say we were relatives of hers. She seemed like an easy target to fulfill the plot of getting my uncles behind bars and turn the whole town against them. The murder of the poor woman, who was known for only doing good in the community, shook the whole town of Mali i Jushit, a town otherwise peaceful where acts such as those were not heard before. Dilë was murdered on a spring night and was discovered dead the following day by a teenage relative who they say he couldn't speak for months after discovering her body. Dilë was lying on the floor covered in blood with her head sliced open like an animal at the butcher. Local communist leaders ordered the whole town to gather near the home of the deceased in the banks of a small creek that runs between the modest houses of the small neighborhood. In the front yard of Dilë's house was a large mulberry tree. Mulberry trees are very common in the town. Besides the mulberry tree, there were lots of wild pomegranate bushes, which are also very common in the area. It was there, at the crime scene, where the gathering took place— for maximum impact. The communists' plan was to be rid of my uncles and in the process silence everyone else by terrorizing them. It worked. At the gathering my uncles were formally accused by one of the members of the Communist Youth, the very group that had planned and executed the murder of the poor woman. Kolë was ordered to be tied to the mulberry tree. Slurs and curses followed by many ignorant young ones and those who wanted him out. Other honest people expressed their disbelief that Kolë would do such a thing, but the communist leaders shut them down quickly to make sure the support for Kolë does not grow further. Most people were afraid to speak up even though they felt sorry for Kolë. There were some brave ones who did speak on his support but were quickly shot down. A dispatch was sent to the police headquarters in Shkodër, and later that evening a military truck with soldiers and policemen arrived. They untied Kolë from the tree and snapped handcuffs on him. They quickly loaded him on the truck and set off to Shkodër.

IV.   Uncle Kolë

Kolë Marash Gjeka was the uncle I never met, but I feel I have been with him for most of his life in Albania following his every step. I have a virtual connection with him and he is definitely my hero. May he rest in peace. When his father died, Kolë was seven years old. He had had a very rough life growing up without a father, but in a small town such as Mali i Jushit, neighbors took care of neighbors, and Kolë had support from male relatives who tried to provide some father figure support. At the time of his arrest, at the age of twenty-three, he was a handsome man with an average built and eagle sharp eyes. He never had any professional athletic training, but was very agile. His hair was combed neatly to one side leaving room for a wide forehead that made him look much more mature than his age. He was known for his sense of humor and love for his family and friends. He played fyell, a primitive type of flute commonly used by shepherds. He didn't shy away from troubles, but those troubles included making fun of someone or taking some figs from the neighbors' fig tree. He did it mostly for the thrill. Like his other siblings, because they had grown up without a father, they were tolerated a little more than a usual kid would. You could say he was a little spoiled but not a criminal. During the war, Kolë had participated in youth underground groups that helped with the

31

fight against Italy and later Germany. Those one-time friends had become his enemies and he stood accused of murder riding on a military truck on the moody roads from Mali i Jushit to Barbullush. As the truck made way to Barbullush and the homes of Mali i Jushit drew farther away, he began to think, *will this be the last time I will see my beloved home?* It was.

After several hours of driving to Shkodër, which had roads full of holes from bombs dropped during the war that had not been paved again, the truck finally pulled in front of the infamous Dega e Mbrendshme.[11] With his hands and legs cuffed he was taken into a dungeon in the basement, and thrown into a one-meter-by-one-meter cell infested with rats and smelling of urine and blood. The walls of the cell were dark red from the blood of the previous tenants and it looked like a bad piece of modern art with paint being spread all over the walls without any visible shape. Here and there, there were writings on the walls: initials, dates, messages that no one could decipher as well as simple love messages left to their loved ones with the hope that someone someday will read. After canvasing the small cell for minutes, he tried to settle and take it all in. This would be his

---

[11] The police headquarters' official name was "Dega e Punëve të Mbrendshme" which translates into Internal Affairs Branch. Other synonyms were shorter forms, such as "Dega e Mbrendshme" or simply "Dega"

residence for the next nine months—and the last one in Albania forever.

Humans hold themselves to the highest standards and proclaim superiority in both intellect and behavior over all other species. We are the self-appointed righteous species. We call someone an *animal* when the person has reached a peak of criminality. How offensive must this be to the animal kingdom? I am not aware of any animal that kills for pleasure. They usually kill their prey to eat it, like a lion kills a deer, or out of fear, when they feel threatened. I also don't know any species that tortures their prey for pleasure. They simply use their power to subdue their prey, but I don't think they take pleasure in hurting another animal. They certainly don't hurt members of the same species for pleasure. Humans, however, do it for pure pleasure. They have done it since the beginning of time and continue to do so today. I would call on the animal rights' activists to advocate for the ban of the name-calling *animal* upon people who have exceeded any limits of cruelty.

Albanian communists did it routinely on political inmates. It was Kolë's turn. For nine months straight, Kolë was tortured in the dungeons of Dega e Mbrendshme. This place was notorious for torturing people arrested and awaiting trial. This was where signed confessions were obtained under tortures for crimes not committed. Those who resisted, even under torture, had their testimonies written and signed for them anyway. Knowing all this, some did resist still out of principal. They would not bear to sign for something they had not done. For nine months, Kolë endured what no one should ever have to. It is almost humanly impossible for anyone to survive under such conditions, but God works in mysterious ways. Besides the frequent beatings, communist monsters used methods that can only be heard of from medieval stories. Mornings started with the interrogations which meant for every question not answered, in his case meant all of them, or answered wrong, he would get beaten up until he lost consciousness. Interrogators would then proceed with putting boiled eggs under his armpits. When that didn't do the job, they stepped it up and removed nails on fingers and toes using pliers until he had none left. Given that in total there are only twenty nails, the whole process must not have taken that long. New methods needed to be used and when they ran out of known ones, they came up with their own. Necessity is the mother of invention. They even cut through his flesh in several places and poured salt on it and then stitched it again. I am not sure who would come up with something like that, but they must be in the best place in hell for sure. Other known and unknown tortures were used systematically, but Kolë did not admit to a crime as heinous as murder that he did not commit. Even though he was in jail accused of murder, most of the interrogation sessions were less about the murder and more about his role in the dissolution of the Kooperativë and collaboration with residence groups to overthrow the regime, which was the real reason he was in jail. They were looking for names of other members, but Kolë didn't give up anyone. Death is terrible, but life with shame is worse. He was not going to betray his comrades and friends. He couldn't possibly give his friends over to these monsters. How could he? Nights and days went by slow. The family back home was anxiously waiting for news on his whereabouts. No one was allowed to visit him and news from the dungeons was scarce.

December 5, 1948; Saint Nicholas eve. The night of Saint Nicholas eve is considered one of the most important days in the Catholic calendar in Albania, after Easter and Christmas. In fact, many non-Catholic Albanians observe this day as well, believing Saint Nicholas to be the protector of Albania. That following day Kolë was scheduled to be hanged. Even though he admitted to no crimes, and no crime could be found, a court was quickly assembled and a sentence was given. Death by hanging was it. The executions were usually commissioned overnight and the city of Shkodër very often woke up to the view of people hanging on trees like victims of cartels on Mexican bridges. Kolë's execution was scheduled for December 6, 1948, but he didn't wait for it in his cell. Kolë was kept constantly handcuffed, even in his fortified one-meter square cell. Most of the time, the guards would tie his legs as well. In the beginning they always tied his legs, but that night he was spared the leg cuffs. He had been tortured for nine months straight, deprived of food, water, and sleep and had been reduced to a walking skeleton. Maybe the guards didn't see much need for cuffing his legs at that point. He was practically dead already. He spent most of that evening praying to Saint Nicholas, after whom he was named as well.[12] He was not praying for his life to be spared for which he was sure it was over but for his family he was leaving behind. He prayed for the evil regime to end soon so the rest of his family would not follow in his footsteps. He prayed for his old mother who had raised him under so much hardship to not collapse at the news of his execution. He prayed for his beloved sister so that she would have a blessed life and not be affected by his deeds. He prayed for his brothers not to follow him into this dungeon or any other dungeons. He prayed for everyone he loved and was loved by to be strong and carry on with their lives. At some point, even though his time on earth was coming to an end and he wanted to stay awake as long as possible, he could not keep his eyes opened anymore and for a brief moment fell asleep. On that brief moment of sleep, he had a dream of Saint Nicholas telling him to escape. While tossing and turning at his

---

[12] Kolë in Albanian means Nicholas.

small cell, he had leaned against the cell door and felt that it had not been locked, so the door cracked open. It was impossible to move a muscle in that cell and not hit the walls of the door somewhere, so his body felt the difference with the opened door. He woke up in disbelief and when he was finally fully awake, he then realized that the guard had forgotten to close his cell the last time he was taken to the restroom that evening. Cells were all situated in the basement of an old building. In order to get out, he needed to walk up the stairs onto the second floor. Walking slowly not to be heard, but also because he was weak, he made it to the second floor undetected. Once on the second floor, where the entrance was heavily guarded, he got out through a window. This description was given to me by my father, who met with Kolë several times. Besides, my father had been at the same dungeon himself shortly after and had a very good visual description of the surroundings. I think he knew the dungeon better than his home. I have not seen nor wish to see this place. The task of getting out of the building on the second floor and jump from a window was not an easy task. With his hands tied, that task seemed just impossible. For someone in his state, a real miracle was needed. And a miracle did happen. In fact, his whole journey was a series of miracles. The will to live is so strong that things that may seem impossible to a normal person are second nature to those who are fighting for their lives. People can gain some powers that are hard for a normal person to understand. But it happens. He got out of the window of the second floor, then, and from there jumped on the roof of the small, two-story house adjacent to the jailhouse. From the roof of the house, he let himself down onto the ground. When my father spoke of this, he used his hands and other gestures and seemed to be walking up those infamous stairs and walking out of that infamous window that I too was following behind Kolë as an invisible ghost. It seemed as I were looking at a hologram of the story. From there Kolë let go and fell on the floor. After a short pause of not making any noise, he almost stopped breathing to ensure no one heard anything. He got up, checked himself for any broken bones, and after ascertaining that he was alright, he started walking. *"A small step for a man, a giant leap for mankind,"*[13] but getting out was only the beginning.

Walk to where, though, is the question? Shkodër is located about thirty kilometers from the closest border crossing to Yugoslavia. A normal healthy person could make it on foot in about five to six hours walking on the road and taking the shortest paths. A person who had been tortured for nine months and without food or water has almost no chance of going anywhere without fainting. Very soon the guards would realize

---

[13] This is the famous quote from Neil Armstrong as he began his walk on the moon after the first moon landing.

he was missing and would set the alarm, which would set a manhunt in motion that was certain to have him back in his cell in no time. His physical appearance was sure to make him identifiable from kilometers away. Even worse, some mad officer might just simply shoot him in the heat if found, or let the dogs do the job for them. No matter how you looked at this, there were no good options for him. With a noose waiting to snap his neck at any moment, Kolë had absolutely nothing to lose. Maybe that was his benefit and inspiration source. Die waiting or die trying; were the only choices he was faced with now. He had no intentions of waiting. His death was almost certain, but he had to try. He was not a quitter. At the very least he was giving these bloodthirsty communist monsters a run for their money. He had no idea what time it was, just that it was night. In his dark dungeon, he hadn't been able to tell days from nights. He had grown so accustomed to dark that the sight of any small light coming from an oil lamp at a house nearby bothered him. He was also tortured with strong lights to cause sleep deprivation. He knew time was not in his favor. Yes, this twenty-three-year-old once a handsome guy with an athletic body that most guys envied and most girls admired, had been reduced into a skeleton from the systematic nine-month inferno, but his mind was sane and most importantly he was convinced that God and Saint Nicholas were with him.

The next daylight found him in a much worse position that he had imagined. By now the guards had realized he was missing and a manhunt was set in motion. His worst fears had come true. His hands were still cuffed. He was wearing a jail uniform and his head was shaved. He was dirty. The only water that had touched his skin had been the one his tormentors had poured in between torturing sessions to bring him alive. It was impossible to blend in and not be identified immediately. Anyone who would see him would recognize him and most likely give him up. He had been walking all night, avoiding roads and any public areas, yet was still too far from the border. On the horizon, he could see the mountains where Albania bordered with Yugoslavia, and it seemed to be at the end of the world. God knows if he even walked on a short path or simply zigzagged his way trying to avoid towns and to not lose direction in these dense forests and swamps. It's hard to tell if he had made any progress in shortening the distance to the "promised land." At that time, there wasn't a real border between Albania and Yugoslavia. One hadn't been established yet because Albanian communists and Yugoslav communists were still in a honeymoon phase of their relationship. He was hoping to pass on the other side of the imaginary border undetected. What would happened after that he was not sure of, as he could have been sent back by Yugoslav communists, yet he had to try because it was his only hope. What did he have to lose anyway? He was somewhere between the city limits of Shkodër and the border of Yugoslavia, in the middle of the fields, still far from his destination and with more people, vehicles, and barking dogs looking for him. The sun was up and people were out and about. He had no chance to go another step with those cuffs around his wrists. Desperation grew, and after a reality check, he knew that he would have to remain where he was, at least until dawn. But he was a sitting duck. When all options are exhausted, turn to prayer. If that doesn't help, it sure doesn't hurt. He got down on his knees like Jesus when he fell with the cross on his shoulders at the Mount Calvary and called on God with a desperate prayer. He prayed to Saint Nicholas one more time and asked for one more favor. He cried for help. His voice was now loud, even though his strength was all gone.

"God! St. Nicholas! You have brought me this far. I believe you want me to live. Please help me get rid of these cuffs!" He cried those words another time and sat down looking at the ground beneath him in despair as if he expected something to come from the ground, or maybe was looking to find the perfect spot to die. He cried and moaned for a short instance and then just sat there motionless. Not sure for how long he had been sitting on that spot, he had passed out because when he woke up, the sun was almost perpendicular to the earth now, an indication that it was close to noon. He woke up to see the cuff on one of the hands loose and he managed to remove the cuffs from one hand still cuffed on the other hand, but that was good enough. God had indeed heard his prayer and performed another miracle.

I believe it was his strong will to live and his hallucination that he believed the miracle happened. It was the fact that he had lost so much weight and that the handcuffs became too loose, perhaps. Or he had pulled the handcuffs with all his force that enabled his hand to slide free. He had put so much force that he was willing to sacrifice one hand to break free. He might have passed out from pain. Kolë was not particularly religious, but he really believed the prayer was heard and a miracle happened. Whatever it was; God almighty, Saint Nicholas, some other saints or gods, or no gods at all, it sure was a miracle. He pulled the cuffs up his arm and hid the other side of the cuffs under his sleeve of the ripped-off jacket. Those who had witnessed his arrival at the Yugoslavian refugee camp had said his left hand was covered in wounds that seemed to be signs of him struggling to remove the handcuffs. We will probably never know how exactly it happened since Kolë is the only person who knew for sure. I think deep down he knew that he worked so hard to remove one hand, yet he attributed that to God, because he was desperate and running out of hope. He had to attribute that to something higher than his being. How else could one believe

42

that a seemingly impossible journey was possible for him? Now with his hands free, he hit the road once again toward the border. Thanking God and Saint Nicholas, empowered with hope and faith that God wanted him to succeed, with police and military with machine guns, armored vehicles and barking dogs storming the area, checking every inch of terrain and leaving no stone unturned, he was on the move again. Up until this time he had been spared being captured, but for how much longer could this go on? Locals were asked to skip work that day and help with the search. Kolë had God on his side and no man can overrun the will of God. Most importantly, Kolë was innocent.

By late afternoon, he had managed to reach the town of Hot, where his mother's family lived. This was the last Albanian town bordering Yugoslavia. Just a few short kilometers ahead lay his last hope, his promised land, his freedom. He knew the area very well because he had spent lots of time there as a child visiting his aunt and roaming with his cousins. He knew every rock, every trail, and every detail of this area. That was his advantage. Most importantly, he knew people he could trust in a day where no one could be trusted. Anyone helping him would have been executed for sure if the regime found out they had helped a fugitive, so anyone helping him took a huge risk. He approached his aunt's home and hid in the bushes near a valley. There he spotted a cousin. He managed to get her attention and give detailed instructions for her father. After a long wait, his cousin returned with food and water and tools to remove the cuffs from the other hand. His cousin brought clothes as well and removed his stinky striped jail uniform. He was rested, fed, clothed, and ready to make the last move. With the help of his cousin, he crossed the border little after dawn. Free at last, but his troubles were far from over for a very long time to follow.

Once in Yugoslavia, Kolë went to look for the house of someone he was related to, Lekë Kola, who happened to live very close to the border. A large portion of Montenegro's land, South Montenegro next to North Albania, is ethnic Albanian population. My other uncle, Gjon, was married to Lekë's daughter, Marë. Kolë knew this family very well and was hoping they could help him. Of course, they were very receptive and hospitable, but at the end they had to turn him over to the Yugoslavian authorities. He was a fugitive after all and an illegal immigrant in this country. Yugoslavia was better than Albania, but it too was a communist country and the closest ally to Hoxha's communist government in Albania. That was about to change soon. Kolë was placed in a refugee camp. Everything happens for a reason or God was simply working solely for Kolë. Whatever the case may have been, Albanian communists went through a nasty divorce and they broke ties with the Yugoslavian leader, Josip Broz Tito, and the two countries that at one time were almost one became enemies and established a border, the same border that many Albanians had fought and died to protect from Yugoslavian land grab. Now Hoxha and Tito had it sorted all out in no time. No shots were fired. Hoxha was thirsty for power and he was not too worried about some lands more or some less, so Tito grabbed whatever he could. What mattered was control and control he got. Breaking from Yugoslavia, the very country that helped him get into power, gave him independence. He was in complete charge now. There were many winners and losers. Albania ultimately lost a large part of its territory and the last nail in the coffin of Albanian isolation was placed, but there was a very clear winner: Kolë. Until then, Yugoslavian authorities had extradition treaty with Albania, and Kolë most likely would have had been turned over to Albanian Authorities. However, the tide turned in Kolë's favor. Even the biggest atheist in the world has to believe in God at least this one time, because I can't explain how all the stars lined up so perfectly in Kolë's favor to the point that the two countries made a deal so fast to make it all work out in his favor. A breakup between the two countries meant Kolë would not be handed over to the Albanians. Kolë could stay in Yugoslavia and not worry about Albanian communists harming him anymore. Kolë's dream started to become more and more possible.

Life as a refugee was not all rosy either, but was heaven compared to communist tortures he endured in Albania. His future was starting to look brighter and he was filled with hope. He let out a deep sigh of relief and went to sleep on his small bed at the corner of the room he shared with several other escapees. That small bed felt like the most luxurious bed at the hotels of Paris or New York. He had forgotten what it means to sleep on a bed. As his eyes closed from the longest journey of his life, so did the darkest chapter of his life.

V.   Uncle Gjekë

My uncle Gjekë was a more laid-back person. He sang and played lahute (lute), one he had built with his bare hands carving it from a mulberry tree. He had little education, only four years, but had learned Italian very well: he was self-taught. Gjekë was not present the day at the town gathering at the horrific scene of Dilë Gjekja's murder, but was soon summoned to appear in Bushat at the municipal police chief's office.

Unlike the big show that was put on to arrest Kolë, Gjekë's arrest was less dramatic. A local auxiliary police officer was sent to arrest him at his home. No trucks, no soldiers, not even handcuffs were used. The person arresting him was a friend and didn't want to cuff him. Gjekë had promised to him that he would obey and not do anything to get him in trouble, so his word was his bond and so it went. Until they reached the police station in Bushat, the only police station in the municipality, which is a long six-kilometer walk, the two of them talked about many things, forgetting the real purpose of that walk. The police officer who escorted him announced his arrival to the chief. Gjekë was then asked to sit and wait in the hallway. After a couple of hours waiting, which seemed like an eternity to him, Gjekë decided to wait no more and took off instead. He managed to run away from custody and went into hiding. His instincts were to walk back toward home, but he knew he could never go home again. Walking with no clear direction, he set for the wilderness close to home. This was an area he knew well and he could hide in caves for some time and try to figure out his next move. He made it into the forest without being caught. As soon as the police chief realized his prisoner-to-be had disappeared, he set a manhunt in motion, and the area was crawling with communists in different uniforms: police, soldiers, communist well-wishers, spies, and just pure bad people with hate in their hearts. For days and weeks, the search operation continued. Family members were interrogated and beaten at their homes. Frightened neighbors shut their doors and hid behind as if the wooden doors would protect them from this fury. Many people were questioned, but no one had any knowledge of his whereabouts. Gjekë knew better than to put his family in danger, so on his way back, he didn't stop at home at all, even though the path to the mountains passed by his home. He went straight to hiding.

For over a year he lived in the wilderness with food supplied by his sister. He couldn't trust anyone else and his sister took a big risk doing that, but what are sisters for? His sister, Nocë, was one of the few people in town who still lived in the mountains and had not embraced the farming lifestyle as most had done long ago. She lived with her husband and two sons in a beautiful valley in a small house built from stones and small windows. In the center, there was a fireplace where all the cooking was done. They owned a goat ranch with which they made a living. They were proud of the mountain life. It gave them a sense of freedom. Almost every day, Nocë would go in secrecy and bring food and clothes to her brother in the small caves more suitable for rats than people, but he was still alive and somewhat free and that was enough for now. After a year in hiding, Gjekë had to figure out his next move. The communists had believed him to be in Yugoslavia by then and he saw no other option but to try to escape to Yugoslavia. These events all took place around the time Kola was preparing for his escape. The two had no contacts or knowledge of each other's plans or whereabouts. Some of these events were pure coincidence.

One winter day in 1949, Gjekë was preparing for his last stand—to take his chance to escape. His sister brought him food and supply for the journey and hugged him for the last time. It was dark. The sun had long set, the stars were brighter than ever, the moon was gold, and the air was cold. In the darkness of night, he left for the Yugoslavian border. If all went well, he would have made it in couple of days. If he were caught, it would be the end of him. He had to be careful, but at least no one was pursuing him and he was not with handcuffs and prison-looking attire. He walked at night and tried to lay low during the day so as not to be seen by anyone. By morning, he had made it to the "Livadet e Shkodrës" (Shkodër Meadows), which is right past the city limits of Shkodër. There he stopped and found a place to hide until dark. He fell asleep for minutes at the time, waking up from any noise. He could never be too careful. Life in hiding had made him paranoid. The sun hid behind the Shkodër Lake again and dark took over. People went home and dogs began to bark. Gjekë started to walk again toward the Yugoslavian border. By morning he made very little progress due to the rough terrain and unknown territory. A few times he had to stop for hours at the time as he had come close to some soldiers guarding the Shkodër Lake, which was considered a border zone. Shkodër Lake was shared between Albania and Yugoslavia and one could swim across. Many had tried. Some had been killed by the Albanian patrols, and very few had managed to get across. Next morning, he stopped again at a forest near Koplik, a citadel in Malsia e Madhe in the northern part of the Shkodër region. The forest was thick and provided with a good hiding place for the day. All he had to do is lay low, be quiet, don't move, and hope no one walked in his direction. Any stranger spotted in this area was a suspect, since Koplik was near the border and the communists treated everyone who had no business being there as an escapee candidate.

Day two went by even slower than the first one since he was unable to sleep at all. He grew wary of the surroundings and the forest didn't help with the constant wood cracking noises from sources he couldn't discern. Now he was not very far from the town of Hot where his aunt's family lived and he had set as destination. The sun set again and clouds covered the stars and moon, but he kept on going in the dark. All night he walked until he reached his aunt's home. It was early morning and his aunt's family were doing their morning chores. Some were letting the sheep out, some milking the cows, and women were cleaning and cooking for the large family. Everyone there loved Gjekë and they were happy to see him. Happy because they loved him, but also happy because for the last year no one knew for sure whether he was alive or dead. They knew he needed help crossing the border, which was not very hard at that point, but it required absolute secrecy. Aiding a fugitive was a risky business, the kind that grants execution or twenty-five years in jail at best. Here was where for the first time in over a year that Gjekë learned of his brother Kolë's whereabouts. Leaving home was hard, but knowing he will have one brother with him, at least, gave him courage and hope. Just the news of Kolë being free made him happy. They welcomed him to the barn, where they kept their sheep, in case someone came snooping around the house during the day. When it got dark, his cousin accompanied him to the other side of the border. Gjekë started walking downhill of Traboini mountain toward Bozhaj.[14] He planned to seek help from Lekë Kola's family, his sister-in-law's family. There he found the same reception as his brother Kolë and proceeded to join him at the refugee camp.

Kolë and Gjekë were free, but from that point on, the Calvary of my family never ended until the fall of Communism in 1992. Kolë and Gjekë escaped, but the end was not even near. This was just the beginning for the rest of the family they left behind. The rest of the family was all punished for the actions of my uncles. All male members of the family were sent to prison at one time or another, some with court sentences and others without any due process. All the women were sent to the internment camps. Some members of the family, such as my father, experienced both.

---

[14] Since this is an Albanian Town that was taken by Montenegro, I will call it by its Albanian name, Bozhaj. In the language of Montenegro, it is spelled Božaj.

VI.   Uncle Nikë

There was a story I heard once that went like this. At the end of the communist regime, a forty-year-old man traveled to a foreign country and his path to the town went through the local cemetery. He was curious to read the headstones and learn a little about this town. What puzzled him was that he read examples such as "Dr. X died three years old," or "Professor Y died five years old." When he arrived in town, he asked how come one can be a doctor at three years old and another a professor at five. They explained to him that in their town they don't write the age of the person when they died but instead summarize the days the person had been happy. Those are the days one really lived. The traveler told them that if he died in their town to please write on his headstone, "Z from Albania. Was born dead." Moral of this story was that Albanian people were never happy during the reign of Communism. Nothing was pleasurable or enjoyable. People were work machines and nothing else. But among them, there were some with even less fortune than others. They had negative happiness equity. On top of all the misery instituted by the regime, there were misfortunes from God. My uncle Nikë was one of them, someone whose headstone would have read "Nikë Marash Gjeka from Albania. He was born dead." Nikë Marash Gjeka was the oldest son of my paternal grandparents.

He was born around the year of 1915. His father, Marash, was in bad health and Nikë had had to take over the reins of the family very early on. His father died when Nikë was only seventeen years old. His father, Marash, died at a young age and left his wife with six children and an old mother. Shortly after his father's death, Nikë got married and had five children. After Kolë escaped from jail and the country, Nikë was arrested and kept in jail for one year without any due process. I don't think he ever even learned why he was there officially, but of course it was a way to make him pay for his brother's escape. The jailers wanted to see if he had any knowledge, or maybe they simply wanted to terrorize him. He was let go without being charged with anything.

VII.   Uncle Gjon

Had he lived in a different era and country, Gjon Marash Gjeka would have been a Perry Mason of sorts. He was so articulate and sharp that even though he had never had any formal education, people used him as defense attorney (until defense attorneys too were outlawed) to defend them in small courts that were established everywhere to punish people for all sorts of things. The so-called judges were bureaucrats without any education of any sort, let alone legal. It didn't really matter, because all they had to do is punish. The only question they had to answer was, how hard? Gjon, thus, had earned himself a reputation for standing up to these peacocks who enjoyed their unearned title of *judge*.

My uncle, Gjon, whom I had been privileged to know very well, since we lived at a house next to his, was a stoic man with many good qualities, but he had little tolerance for lies and deceits and didn't do well in hiding his emotions toward the regime. He was a handsome strong man with wide shoulders, and a great smile—if he could manage to smile, that is, because most of the time he was serious but friendly. Because I never met my grandfather and Gjon was much older than my father, I looked at him as a grandfather; he was happy to oblige. Gjon had no kids of his own and we all loved him and he loved us all. He was known for his public speaking skills and for someone who had never attended a school, he had great knowledge of geography, history, and could write and read and do simple arithmetic. He had memorized the whole "Lahuta e Malcis" — "The Lute of Highlands": the voluminous epic works of Gjergj Fishta. All this on top of his litigation skills. Gjon was the second-born son of my paternal grandparents. His father died when Gjon was only fourteen years old. As a result, he had to mature a lot earlier. Gjon was married to a woman from Bozhaj, a town that after the new borders were drawn, fell on the Yugoslavian side. After that, his wife was a foreigner in Albania as far as the communist regime was concerned. After Kolë's escape, Gjon was arrested and interrogated for thirteen months without any due process and then released without being officially charged nor sentenced. I guess he had nothing to offer the regime they didn't already know at the time, or God knows how the authorities felt that day to let him go. Maybe thirteen months of torture were just enough, for now, as they could bring him back anytime they felt like.

Marë, Gjon's wife who was from Bozhaj, which fell under Yugoslavia, after the new borders were drawn, was given two choices. One, leave her husband and return to Yugoslavia, or two, stay in Albania with no rights to ever go back and see her family. She chose the latter and never saw her family again, until

1991. Marë didn't have any kids and the only person she was related to in the entire country was her husband. She was not allowed to see her family, and most of the family she knew had already died of age when she was allowed to visit again in 1991, despite the distance of less than fifty kilometers. Her only crime was the fact that she had decided to marry my uncle, while, unbeknownst to her, this town would become a different country. She left as a young girl of seventeen and returned an old woman of sixty-four years. Her brother had been seven when she got married and now he was fifty-four. She didn't know anyone, and the house she grew up in seemed strange to her. Great disappointment covered her whole being and she cried profusely. All the time of dreaming to go back were repaid by a great disappointment. Her family, as she had known it, was no more. Her house, as she had known it, was no more. Her hometown was estranged to her. She felt she didn't belong there. She couldn't wait to come back to her husband and his family, which included me, the only family she had known.

VIII.   My Father

My father, Zef Marash Gjeka, was the youngest of his siblings and was only four years old when his father died. He was raised by his mother and grandmother and with father figure support from his older brothers, most of whom were not much older than him. His youth was uneventful apart from the usual hardships of the time. During the war he had tried to help with youth groups in fighting Nazis. Their fights, being very young, consisted of passing messages between guerrillas, bringing them food occasionally, or other small chores. At the end of the war, he was sixteen years old and ready and eager to serve in the military. Zef was stationed in the coastal city of Vlore, in the south, and was part of the unit that established the first coast guard branch, making sure Albanian coasts on the Adriatic and Ionian seas were closely watched.

While young Zef was proudly defending the costs of Albania, his family back home had become target of the communist government. His two brothers had escaped and they were now considered enemies. Barely twenty years old, Zef came home discharged from the military service after surviving a disease that almost killed him and escaped a sure amputation of his left leg by some miracle and by some even braver doctors. Instead of receiving a veteran's welcoming, he was sent to an internment camp with his entire family. Cause: he was the brother of Kolë and Gjekë who had dared escape the country. The family at the time consisted of my grandmother Marukë; my uncle Nikë with wife Lulë and two-year old son, Mark; uncle Gjon and his wife Marë; and my father Zef. My aunt Nocë was married and lived with her husband and sons nearby. They were spared the persecution. Gjon and Nikë were both in jail. Now the rest of the family—grandmother Marukë; father Zef; two aunts, Lulë and Marë; and my cousin Mark—were all headed for a new home in the Tepelenë internment camp. One early morning they woke up to knocks at the door from the secret police who ordered them to take their personal belonging and get in a military truck that was surrounded by lots of soldiers and police and God knows who else. The display of power was as if the military had caught the biggest terrorists. These were the most innocent and most vulnerable members of the family, yet the regime could care less and without any remorse loaded them into military trucks like sardines in a can and sent them to the infamous Tepelenë internment camp, which was more like a concentration camp. The internment camp my family was sent to was close to a jail. It had earned the nickname of the Albanian Auschwitz. These people had done nothing wrong. Their only crime was that they were related to two young innocent guys who escaped atrocities of a brutal communist regime installed and executed by the barbarians of Albania. After repeated requests made to the higher commands of the camp and even the dictator himself, my father was allowed to return home after a year in the internment camp, due to a special ordinance based on his military service, whereas the rest of the family were kept for three years. Government sequestered two fifths of the property, taking away the part that would have belonged to my uncles who escaped. The property was split in five, accordingly, since there were five male members, and two parts were sequestered. To make up for the part of the home and land, the family had to pay in cash so government would not take two fifths of the house and land as well. They were broke, but became even more so. Money had to be borrowed from friends and relatives to pay for those high fees imposed on the price of the house and land. Ironically, shortly after the entire land would be confiscated anyway and become government property: Kooperativë.

Once the entire family returned home from internment camps and jails, they regrouped and tried to make sense of their new life and plan the next move. There was very little to figure out. Their lives under the communist regime would never be easy again. My father, now of age for marriage, started planning to build his own family. According to the tradition, marriages were mostly arranged. Good family names and other criteria played a high role in that society. Ironically, these people lived in the greatest poverty, yet their mindset was stuck in some virtual aristocracy. They carried themselves as if they were the direct descendants of Queen Teuta[15] or Skenderbeu.[16] My father's family had nearly nothing. They had had nothing from a very long time. Now they had less than nothing. They had no titles, lands, or anything to distinguish them. Somehow, they thought so highly of themselves that only someone of equal standards would be a good fit. Their pride was unparalleled as it was the case with all highlanders at the time. As per my mother, her family was a little better in some aspects. They had owned lots of land and livestock for many years and had built a comfortable life. My grandfather had been appointed the chieftain (equivalent of mayor) of his town, Shënkoll (Saint Nicholas) in the Lezhë district, for many years. But even my mother's family, like most well-to-do families, was the target of communists. My mother, a young girl at the time, with all the dreams of marrying a well-to-do handsome man, was handed a marriage proposal by my father. My father had nothing to offer besides his charm. That did it for her. As things were looking, no one would have anything left shortly after, so my mother's

---

[15] Teuta was a famous Queen who ruled the Shkodër Castle in ancient times when that part of Albania was called Illyria.

[16] Gjergj Kastrioti, also known as Skenderbeu, was a medieval leader who fought the Ottoman Empire and succeeded to keep the country free for twenty-five years until his death. He is considered to be the greatest leader Albania has ever had. Modern Albanians call themselves descendants of Skenderbeu as an honorary portrayal of his greatness.

father agreed to the marriage proposal, and my parents were engaged. Under the communist regime, other classes were formed: pro-Communism people and against-Communism people. The pro-Communism class would not marry anyone on the other side, so my mother's options were limited now. Their aristocratic titles meant nothing anymore. What mattered now was which side you were on. And the imaginary titles from the highlands were of course always kept close like the exiled kings parade in foreign lands with no subjects of their own. My father seemed as good a choice as any. Engagements, arranged or not, are a happy time. Girls spent their time at home most of the time until they got married; so all girls were excited by the change. My mother didn't have much say on the matter, but she was happy with the idea of marrying a man. As to which man, it didn't matter. It was a mission-accomplished kind of feeling, a life milestone, a job well done for her. Wedding plans were set in motion and both families were excited. What followed next, it turned out, would be anything but celebration.

Albanians weren't able to overthrow the communist regime for many years, not for the lack of trying, but I'm sure they must have been cursed. People of all ages and professions tried and failed. They organized underground resistances, opposition groups, armed groups, and even created alliances with foreign governments, but all their attempts went in vain. My father's family had already been destroyed and he was not going to die without a fight. He managed to contact other opposition groups and become a member of the underground world working to overthrow the regime. My uncle Kolë, who was now in Yugoslavia, had been training as a volunteer to enter Albania and help organize uprisings.

I don't want to speculate on a topic I'm not informed on, but there are unproven theories that the Yugoslavian secret service (UDB) used people like Kolë to enter Albania for their own purposes. Kolë was eager for revenge and whatever the real UDB's mission might have been, he was happy to use them as a vehicle to accomplish his goals. A win-win situation, I think. I will leave this to historians, as I am not equipped with the necessary knowledge to claim UDB's intentions or methods.

In any event, the communist regime had a special name for these people. They were called "diversant," another non-Albanian word with no real meaning in Albanian, used to identify people who escaped and were entering the country to assist local resistance groups. Sometimes the government would make up stories of some diversant groups entering Albania, just to persecute someone.

Kolë participated in many missions that intended to destabilize the Albanian regime and assist local resistance. Their small units, made up of escapees in collaboration with guerrillas

even born yet, this event marked another sentence on my future life. Being born from this man would put a target on me as well whenever I am to be born. The torture place and period was called the "Hetuesi," which meant "the investigation." This was not the investigation, but the admitting of crimes under duress. The case had been drafted beforehand and all they did here is torture the inmate to admit. After many months of interrogation and tortures, he had signed an affidavit that included all the charges brought upon him. My father used to say, "I was guilty as charged, but I don't feel guilty for fighting Communism."

Sometimes you can find light even in the darkest places, such as a flower that blossoms in a desert. In the most unlikely of times and places, such as the dungeons of Shkodër's Dega e Mbrendshme, my father found his guarding angel. While he was awaiting trial, the officer in charge of the investigation—"the torture master" would be more apt—was abruptly transferred and in his place a young officer was brought in. The young officer, a big-hearted man, then, took away the signed affidavit and handed my father a blank paper. The original signed affidavit could have sent my father to death, but he was given a second chance. The new modified affidavit was completed with this officer's help where some of the very damaging testimony was removed. Letting him completely off was not an option, but sparing his life was all he could do. His trial, typically one-sided, was completed in a day and my father received a sentence of fifteen years in jail and the sequestration of property: his share, whatever was left of it, and a ban on voting rights for three years after jail, even though Albania had a one-party ruling government and voting meant nothing. The terms Party and Government were used interchangeably. Ever since I have become eligible to vote I have never missed an opportunity to vote. Vote should be sacred for every person in a free society, but for me it has an additional meaning. It is a tribute to my father. He didn't have an attorney because defense attorneys were outlawed, but the modified signed affidavit had been weakened and instead of getting the maximum sentence prescribed by the law, which was death, he received a lesser sentence. Maximum sentences were more likely in communist courts, then anything less. The minimum sentence was ten years in prison. The Albanian penal code, article 64,[17] prescribed a minimum of ten years to death for such crimes and always confiscation of property. Communist judges enjoyed executing their undeserved power they had over unprotected civilians and didn't hide their disgust for them. For the next eight years, my father moved from one hard labor camp to another working as a slave of the regime. He endured what was widely accepted as

---

[17] "Kodi Penal i Republikës Popullore të Shqiperisë i vitit 1952"—Penal Code of Peoples' Republic of Albania, 1952.

the new norm. Communist jails came in different flavors. There was one called the "Burgu i Burrelit"—Burrel Prison where the most sworn enemies of Communism were sent. This was the kind of white-collar crime jail without the amenities, the kind where you would find the elite of the pre-communist society. Here, you would find the most educated class. This infamous place was the inferno of all jails. It had a one-way entry. No one was ever supposed to come out alive. No one ever did, in fact, until the political prisoners were freed in 1990 as a result of pressure by the West and from the impending fall of Communism. The welcome sign at the entry read, "Burgu i Shfarosjes": the prison of extermination. Most inmates received twenty-five-year sentences, and as they got closer to completing the sentence, another was handed down by the jail command— and then another. In other words, it was made sure no one left alive. One good thing about this jail was the fact that the inmates were not forced to work as in other places. These political prisoners were considered way too dangerous to trust them with working and potentially escaping. My father was not that lucky, I guess, to make it here, or maybe too lucky because he made it out alive. Depending on the day, he may have switched his thinking between feeling lucky and unlucky. He was sent to work at the major projects of the time such as building the only airport in the country, Rinas, and draining the swamps of

Myzeqe. Myzeqe is a large area: a coastline where the Adriatic and Ionian seas meet. It is a large area below sea level; a mosquito's heaven and a man's nightmare. Malaria was way too common and the moisture in the air exceeded any known acceptable levels. Work and living conditions were inhumane and beating and torturing was never in short supply, but food and water always was. The government had decided to drain the water and use the land for farming. This wasn't a bad idea in principle, however, but it was done using slave labor. The Communist Party bragged about their achievements and these major projects day and night, but left out the details of slave labor from prisoners, internees, and so-called volunteers. These slave projects for my father were a product of unjustified persecution, a young man with dreams cut short, a man who fought hard to survive this misery for eight very long years.

I don't know where these people found the strength or motivation, but they had such a strong will that they beat all the odds and defied all the laws of physics. Many people weren't able to survive and died in these camps though, and their families weren't even allowed to bury their bodies. The dead were buried in common graves. Back home, my father had an old mother, a sick brother with his family who tried to save all they could to send food to him in jail, and a second brother with his wife who tried to maintain what was left of their family together. Each inmate had to complete a certain amount of work per day, the "norm." The amount assigned was such that any normal person would have a very hard time to complete. Malnourished and overworked inmates would have had even harder time to complete the norm. I can't even begin to imagine. The will to live is so strong that it can sometimes push humans beyond their boundaries. There was a policy established that if an inmate managed to complete two norms, then they would get a day subtracted from their sentence. I don't know how he did it, or how many of those norms my father must have completed, but somehow he got his sentence reduced by four years. Sometimes Hoxha would give amnesty to inmates on major holidays or special occasions, usually criminals and thieves, but not the political prisoners such as my father. Usually, Hoxha would free a category of people with small sentences left to serve, or reduce sentences for another category. In one instance, my father was part of this category and he received an amnesty on an occasion when the dictator must have been drunk or under some other influence or narcotics where he was forgiven another three years. His sentence was now cut almost in half. From the original sentence of fifteen, he served eight years. He was released in the spring of 1961.

At thirty-five years of age, Zef was let go home after having given the last drip of his blood to the communist sharks. His four years of service to his country in the military, one year internment camp, and eight years of prison had changed the man so much that he didn't recognize himself, his family even less. Once a full of live boy with a handsome appearance and an athletic body, he was reduced to an old man more suitable for a sixty-five-year-old man. His body was exhausted, but his spirit was unbroken. He still had hope.

IX.   Uncle Gjergj

Most species, as far as I know, have separate roles between males and females: mothers and fathers. For the most part (there are some species with alternate roles), mothers are the nurturing and caring gender and the fathers are the providing and protecting gender. A mother does anything to nurture her offspring: take food from her own mouth, cover them with her body to keep them warm while shivering herself, and in some rare species, a mother will even feed its own young with its own flesh (usually skin). Fathers, on the other hand, do anything to protect their tribe by fighting off the predators and providing food for them. They fight off even the most frightening beasts and even die. They die protecting their tribe but don't abandon them. They know their duty. Animals do it all the time, and for humans, the roles are no different, even though in modern times we have adapted to sharing and doing things together, but our instincts have not changed. Women are the nurturing and caring gender, even though modern life has given them other responsibilities. Despite what their daily jobs entail, men are still the hunters and gatherers and the protectors of their families. The most sacred duty for a man is to protect his family. I can't imagine the anguish of a father who has been forced to abandon his family. I don't know where he can find the courage to continue living when he is eternally separated by his wife and kids. Is it hope? Is it the will to live that supersedes any other human emotions and feelings and even the most basic natural instinct that is to protect his family? Do we, as humans, really love our kids more than ourselves as we claim, or have we not been put to test to prove? I certainly don't know, but some of the events of this tale supersede my ability to apprehend how any of this could be possible. And yet it is. Perhaps we humans are driven by other feelings such as honor. A man can sacrifice himself, his family, and everything dear to him in order to preserve honor. What is life worth if it is not lived with honor and dignity? The answer is clear, even though the outcome is still ruthless, but social norms are created for a reason and most people chose to obey: that is what separates humans from animals, I guess. This is where heroes and villains are different. Other species in the animal kingdom could care less about honor, heroes or villains.

Following the examples of their masters from the Russian Revolution who exterminated a whole class of educated and wealthy people, the Albanian communist machine was set in motion very early on, and without wasting any time they went immediately after big families, the educated class, and anyone with anything. Dedë Zef Radi, my maternal grandfather, was the patriarch of a large family who owned land in one of the best areas for farming in Shënkoll, in the region called Bregu i Matit in the Lezhë district. Bregu i Matit means Mat riverbank. Bregu i Matit comprises many small villages and Shënkoll is the center of it. Shënkoll is located at the triangle of the Mat river and Adriatic Sea. The sun rises over the mountains of Krujë and sets on the Adriatic Sea creating a spectacle on most sunny days and even on some cloudy and rainy days full of rainbows. The area is a large flat land perfect for farming and livestock. Heavy rains cause the Mat river to flood the lands nearby several times a year. While the flooding itself is not desirable; the locals had built their homes on high grounds safe from flooding; the result is a farming paradise as the river leaves behind a composition of leaves and manure it brings from the mountains where it originates.

The large Radi family had enjoyed living in riches for decades under different governments that ruled Albania since the Ottoman Empire and for the most part their lives hadn't changed much. They were left alone to farm and pay taxes. Taxation was applied to one tenth of their products. Pretty generous I would say and so did they. Most of the land was owned by several well-to-do families and they hired help year round to work in their farms and ranches who were well compensated and, in most cases, the workers had homes provided to them free of rent in the farm or ranch. Help was never in short supply as people from the mountains were constantly in the lookout for an easier life than the one in the mountains where resources were scarce and winters were harsh. There were also some who owned enough land to make a good living, but had to work it themselves. They were neither rich nor poor. They were, to use the common phrase, in the middle class. They made good living for themselves as well. A lot of workers purchased small pieces of land with their salaries over time and they too became landowners, and so the cycle continued.

Life was good for a long time for everyone. My grandfather's family lived in a very large house with many amenities of a typical aristocratic house at the time. Running a farm, even with all the help, required lots of work and management from its owners, such as finances, payroll, etc., in addition to possessing a great deal of knowledge about agriculture, soil, climate, crops, and seeds. My uncle Gjergj Radi was the person who was a well-known connoisseur of agriculture and had a passion for farming, although he had never had any education or special training in the field. Growing up on a farm and living there his entire life had prepared him to take over the role of agriculture specialist of the family farm.

Gjergj was the first-born son of Dedë Zef Radi and File Dodja. He was born on March of 1923. The birth of a son, especially the first one, was a special event and celebrations lasted for weeks where family, friends, and it was customary for well-wishers to stop by to bring gifts for the newborn. Gunshots were heard day and night as groups of people coming to congratulate would fire their guns as they approached the Radi estate, another widely used tradition at the time. While I don't know the genesis of this custom, I believe it meant to symbolize the addition of another gun, another soldier. This old tradition comes from the ancient times when all men had to be ready in case of war—and wars were never ending. This was a typical patriarchal society where a son was a king. Firing a gun also occurred at weddings and other celebratory occasions.

Like most of his peers in Bregu i Matit, he grew up in a large family with uncles, aunts, and lots of cousins. They spent winters in their farmhouse and summers in the mountains where they had a summer house. Hired help managed the farm and a male member of the family would stay behind to supervise. The adult males of the family took turns spending summers at the farm, something they never looked forward to doing. Gjergj grew up to be a respected young man who had good manners and understood and observed traditions. Nonetheless, he had a great sense of humor and he could tell a joke at the even most depressed mode. In 1942, at the age of nineteen—an age considered appropriate for marriage—and being the oldest son, he had to marry as per tradition. The family had set eyes on one of the girls from a very prominent family in the area. The two families agreed and Gjergj was engaged to Prenë, the daughter of Prekë Tom Tahiri. Prekë Tom Tahiri was one of the biggest landowners in the area and had a very good family name. He would be labeled *kulak* later on by the regime. Kulak is a mispronounced and misunderstood version of the Russian word *Gulag*. Unlike a gulag (internment camp) of which there were many in Russia, kulak was simply a label meant to denigrate the class of landowners. So many people who didn't even own a lot of land were labeled as kulak as well when the regime didn't like them and no other crime could be found. It was an easy win. Being labeled as a kulak had a very similar connotation to villain. Propaganda made sure to vilify kulaks as ruthless slave owners who mistreated their workers. The truth was far from it.

The mini-aristocracy was still well alive. During World War II, the Radi family had supported the legalists (ex-King Zog supporters). Their home had become a safe haven for guerrilla leaders and soldiers alike. Occasionally, partisans and even Italians and Germans were harbored as well as a Christian duty and as Albanian tradition requires that no one is turned back when they seek help. At the end of World War II in 1945, Gjergj was recruited and joined the military. He was assigned to the very distinguished "Brigada e Parë Sulmuese"—First Offensive Brigade. The military was still managed under wartime structure and soldiers were still called partisans. This brigade was commanded by none other than Mehment Shehu, who was one of the main communist figures to lead the partisan guerrillas during World War II and infamously prosecute the anti-communists during and after the war. Gjergj served the mandatory time and in 1947 was discharged. On March 26, 1948, the newly married couple was blessed with the birth of a son, Llesh. Things had changed drastically since he had left home and his family had become a target for owning land but also for having supported non-communist factions such as the Legalists and Ballists. Communists labeled anyone with any possessions bourgeois, so it was a matter of time when this family would find itself the target of the communist regime. Gjergj tried to lay low and not get mixed up with anything that would attract any attention, focusing on running the family business. Since the agrarian reform of 1946, the taxes on farmers had been raised so much that in some cases the land didn't even produce enough to simply pay the taxes. The taxes were not a percentage of a farms' product or based on profit, but a finite amount of products: it was a shopping list with defined amount. A farmer had to work and pay taxes, and if anything was left, they could keep it. Farmers couldn't even choose what to grow, since the new tax reform required specific products be given to government. For instance, if you wanted to grow corn, but the

79

tax tally required wheat, you had to grow wheat just for the taxes. Farmers didn't really own their land anymore for all intents and purposes. This was the last push toward the state-owned farming Kooperativë, which was the real goal that was achieved later on by making the communist regime the only landowner in the country. On May 6, 1950, a second son, Pal, was born and soon the family was growing and prospering.

In 1951, Gjergj was summoned to appear in Capital Tirana at the office of the Agriculture Ministry. Since he was someone with knowledge and passion for agriculture and was well known in the area, he thought he was being offered some kind of a government job. Albania was predominantly agricultural and modernization of the sector was in dire need. *I will make a difference*, he thought the whole time during his long trip to the capital. He entered the offices of Agricultural Ministry and announced himself. A young woman with a pale face and short hair at the front desk told him to wait. He sat there impatiently rubbing his knees and fixing his necktie making sure it was straight and aligned. After a long wait, a thin man appeared. He was so thin it seemed he would fold in two as he walked. He was wearing a suit two sizes bigger held by a belt tight around his waist and a crooked tie on a large white shirt. His black shoes were very shiny and his hair was neatly combed. He looked like a manikin staring at an empty Italian cloth store window. It was obvious that he was proud of his new job that had him wear a suit, something he clearly had never worn before. He put on a fake smile and greeted Gjergj and told him that he was needed at the Interior Ministry instead where Mehment Shehu, once his army commander, wanted to see him. Shehu had become the Interior Minister now. He was one of the most ruthless criminals of the regime who had committed the most heinous crimes against the Albanian population during and especially after the war. He executed many anti-communists without any due process, usually in front of everyone at the town squares or shot them on the head on the spot. Eventually in 1981, Mehmet Shehu had fallen out of favor with his own party and was eliminated. He was found dead on his bed, shot in the back. The official statement was that he had committed suicide, but later investigations pointed to an execution from the secret police. The days following his death, the government charged him posthumously with treason and his entire family was locked at the infamous Burrel jail where the sworn anti-communists were serving their sentences, mostly sent by Shehu himself. Karma, I guess. He will not be missed.

Walking through the corridors of the government building, many thoughts ran through his head. *Why would he have called me? Will he offer me a job? What can I do for the interior ministry? I am just a farmer.* But his puzzle was soon solved. As

81

he entered one of the rooms, he had no idea where he was, but was told it was the office of the minister. However, the minister was not there, but Gjergj was approached by two men from the secret police who grabbed him without giving any explanation and took him to another room that was dark and frightening. Several secret police officers and agents in plain clothes came and went from that room for ten days, one offering coffee, water, or food and the others offering him a glimpse view of what would become of Albania: terror. He was asked to become an informant and work for the secret police by ratting on his family, friends, and anyone who the regime would want to target. Gjergj Radi wouldn't do such thing. The idea alone made him want to vomit. He had grown up on a respected family where *Besa*[18] was the most important trait. His family had harbored friends and foes in times of need and never betrayed anyone. How could he do that? When the god cop/bad cop methods didn't work on him, his tormentors changed to the methods they knew best: beating and torturing. This went on for ten days. He was let go with one order: "Think about it and let us know! If you work with us, your life and that of your family will be bright. The Party will take care of you. If you don't, you will rot in jail. Your family will be sent to an internment camp and jail."

---

[18] Besa is a typical world used to describe the sacred promise a person makes. It means *my word is my bond*. According to ancient Albanian customs, Besa cannot be broken.

Since he didn't return home and didn't send any word to the family, the family was worried sick. They tried to contact local government officials and anyone they could think of, but no one had any knowledge of his whereabouts. After ten days, he came home. Not only had they beaten and tortured him, but I don't think they even fed him at all, because when he came home, his family didn't recognize him. He had lost so much weight and was traumatized. The whole trip from home to Tirana had been an episode of daydreaming about becoming this big shot in the Albanian Agriculture Ministry, but his return trip was filled with rage, anger, and anxiety for his future and that of his family. What now?

After he returned, he could never be the same anymore. He didn't speak to anyone for months and didn't even tell his family what had happened. He was in shock and disbelief. How could the government of his country he just served for three years do this to him? What could he do now? He wasn't sure, but one thing he knew way too well was that he was not safe in Albania anymore. Gjergj had never envisioned leaving his home. Especially now that he had a wife and two sons. His father was old and a double amputee from a bone eating disease. His father's second wife and her young son needed him as well. His sisters were young and needed support. He was the head of the family. So many people depended on him. But more importantly, he was well aware of the consequences of his escape, were he to make that terrible decision.

One day he finally opened up to his family of what had happened. He confessed to the adults over dinner. After discussing at length with his father and uncles, they all agreed that he had to save himself and the family would be ok. He was young and full of life, and staying home meant he had two choices: work for the communist regime and spy on his people, or be jailed. Neither of those choices would have a happy ending. This is where humans supersede other animals, which have no regard for morals. This is where heroes and villains are separated. This is where history books are written. His family would have been prosecuted anyway if he disagreed to cooperate, so at least he had to save himself. He didn't want to believe the choices he had or the advice he was getting, but deep down he knew this was the new reality.

After thinking for weeks, he made his decision. "I will not become another victim of Communism nor will I become their enabler," he decided. After that night, all he was thinking was about the plan to escape the country. That was not an easy task and required the utmost secrecy. He confessed to his father and his uncles his decision, but made them swear to not tell anyone, not even his wife. He knew that he couldn't bear seeing her after she learned about his plan. Other people in the area, friends and relatives, had been targeted by the regime and several of them wanted to escape as well. He joined the group of five and set to leave the country toward Yugoslavia. Since they had lived near the Mat river and the Adriatic Sea their whole lives, they were good swimmers, so they thought that the best way was to cross the borders was via the Buna river. Buna is a very narrow deep river that is also the borderline between Albania and Yugoslavia that has claimed many lives over the years: lives of people trying to escape. From Shënkoll to Buna it is about forty kilometers. The river was heavily watched during the summer, when swimming was more probable, but during the fall and winter, when swimming wasn't suitable, it was less watched. Also, nights are longer during the fall and there is more dark time. The group of five left their homes, without many goodbyes apart from some close confidants, and on October 15, 1951, around midnight, they made it to Buna riverbanks. Once at the riverbanks, having past all the military and police checkpoints undetected, they made the sign of cross and said a short prayer, then removed all their clothes and tied them around their wastes in small plastic bags. Filled with anxiety and hope, they entered the freezing waters of the Buna. The currents of the river are always strong, but after heavy rains they are even stronger and the water levels are much higher.

All five of them entered Buna at the same spot, but were quickly split and no one could see the others. It was every man for himself. They had no equipment or waterproof clothing. All they had was youth courage, hope, and faith in God. They had grossly underestimated Buna. This wasn't like swimming in the Adriatic during the day in known shallow calm waters. This was not like swimming in the currentless Mat, which is as calm as the Pacific Ocean. Buna is a different kind of body of water, the killing type. Their bodies floated away like fallen leaves in cold waters and the strong currents of Buna. After an hour in the water, Gjergj found himself on the other side of the water many kilometers west of his entry point. He was shivering and short of breath, but somehow a sense of happiness brought warmth to his body. However, the rough water had stolen his bag of clothes. He thanked God for having taken him alive on Yugoslavian land and started to look around for his comrades. He called their names one at the time, but no answer came. He walked up and down the riverbanks looking for them and calling their names, but nothing, just pure silence, which was only interrupted by the splashes of water hitting the curves of riverbanks and an occasional wood log making way toward Adriatic. He sat and tried to take cover in a small cave, but didn't stay long. He started to call his friends names again and again, until one of them answered. This was his cousin and best friend Fran Kola.

Now two of them joined forces looking for the others, but there were nowhere to be seen nor heard.

After hours of desperate search, they had to leave or die from hyperthermia. The sun would have risen soon over the Albanian Alps of Shkodër as well, and they had to move before sunlight. They canvased the area one more time in hopes of seeing their friends, to no avail. The town of Shtoj,[19] in Yugoslavia, was nearby and the people living there are all Albanians. Gjergj and Fran walked for several minutes and reached the nearest home. They called "O i Zoti i Shpise," *Hey, owner of the house,* as it is the tradition. Dogs started barking everywhere. A man came out and invited them in. All the family members woke up and offered them food and clothes and set up something for them to sleep. In the morning, they were handed to the authorities, as that was the rule, but this family had fulfilled their Christian duty and the Albanian tradition. Gjergj and Fran were sent to a refugee camp in Ulqin and days later they learned that the bodies of the three traveling companions, their relatives and friends, had washed up onto the Ada beach: a small island created where the Buna forks before finally setting free the massive body of water into the Adriatic Sea. Gjergj and Fran cried like children at the news of the loss of their friends and cursed at the communist

---

[19] Since this is an Albanian town that was taken by Montenegro, I will call it by its Albanian name, Shtoj. In the language of Montenegro, it is spelled Štoj.

regime that had forced them to take this dangerous voyage. Gjergj was safe, physically, but his heart would never heal again. He left behind his pregnant wife, Prenë, and his young sons, Llesh and Pal.

Even though the infrastructure and communications were very much inexistent, the news still traveled fast. The family was somewhat relieved, but also anxious of what would come next. His wife Prenë was devastated, even though she did understand and forgave him. They never did see each other again. Gjergj started his life as a refugee and Prenë's endless life of hardship began.

Two months had passed since Gjergj's escape and his wife Prenë gave birth to a girl. They named her Vitore (Albanian for Victoria), which means victory. Vitore would never meet her father. It didn't take long for the communist beast to unleash its evil on the family of Gjergj, and as it was to be expected, someone would be sent to the internment camp. The twofold question was who and where? In a matter of few short months after the birth of Vitore, Prenë and the little girl were sent to the Tepelenë internment camp. Gjergj's relatives took in the two boys. They were separated from their father, mother, and little sister, but they were at least spared the brutal life of Tepelenë Camp, which has been called the Albanian Auschwitz by survivors. It was hard for anyone and especially for a newborn.

Vitore's fragile body eventually gave up at eighteen months. I don't know how Prenë managed to keep her alive that long in that camp where even the strongest of men have given up. Vitore died without ever really having been alive. Her body was buried somewhere in the camp in an unmarked common grave, as it was the case with everyone who died in the camp. Vitore was the youngest victim of communist atrocities against the Radi family, a family that had devoted their lives to God, family, and helping others. They chose honor over self-preservation. Prenë completed the three-year sentence in a life filled with misery, and many times heartbroken, but somehow found the courage to live and carry on. She came home and united with her toddler boys she had not seen in three years. Her heart was in pieces, but her morale was high. She decided to raise the boys on her own.

Gjergj tried to make a life in Yugoslavia and settled in the city of Ulqin where majority of the population is Albanian and he had some distant relatives living there as well. On top of that, his close friend and cousin, Fran, was with him as well. At least they had each other. Farming skills were not needed here, so he learned carpentry and found work around the city of Ulqin making a decent living working hard and keeping his head down.

During the 1960s and '70s, many people from there migrated to United States. At the same time, Enver Hoxha had issued an amnesty to those who had escaped and wanted to return home, promising no retaliation and full pardon, provided they had no blood on their hands. Some people fell into the trap the evil dictator had laid and believed his word. Upon return, they were met by secret police who sent them straight to jail and executed them. Gjergj was visiting his brother Gjeto in Italy and asked him for advice. Gjeto was an exiled Catholic priest and had spent his entire life in schools in Rome. He was a very educated man. Gjergj had believed this lie and maybe part of him simply wanted to believe because he wished to return home to his family. Not only did Gjeto not trust the regime, he was convinced that this was a trap, so he told his brother that his only way was to migrate to United States because he was done with Albania forever. Gjergj had never said goodbye to his family. He had hoped that he would one day return after the regime fell, but now that day seemed very distant. Taking his brother's advice, he wrote a letter to his family where he finally did say goodbye. Gjergj migrated to New York in United States joined by Fran Kola. They lived close by in New York as well. Gjergj found work as carpenter and made a good living in New York and saved up to send money to his family, but the regime didn't allow it. Gjergj died on January 27, 1983, and was buried in the small town of Shtoj in Ulqin, Yugoslavia. His last wish had been to be buried in Albanian soil. Because he wasn't allowed to be buried in the country of Albania, Shtoj had been his second choice being that Shtoj is Albanian soil as well. After the fall of Communism, his remains were brought to his final rest in his beloved Shënkoll where he was born and raised.

X.   Uncle Gjeto

When religion was again legalized in Albania, after it had been banned for twenty-two years, my mother had wanted me to become a Catholic priest. Albania had very few surviving priests who were mostly old and there was a need for priests, but I admit, I am not that brave. I would dismiss her: "Your brother was a priest. Don't you think this family has given enough to church? And where is he? No one even knows about him." She did leave me alone eventually, because as she believed, "one has to feel it, not be forced or manipulated in any way. It must be a personal choice." I was fourteen when my mother was trying to persuade me to dedicate my life to the church, but my uncle, Gjeto Radi, was only six years old when he decided to become a priest and dedicate his life to the church and Christ. In fact, he had it all figured out: a Franciscan missionary priest. I'm not sure where he got the idea as young as he was, but the decision he made at six years old became a reality, even though the path was very bumpy. Sometimes fate is decided before one is even born, it seems. Before Christianity, Albanians were Pagans and had their own gods. There's a very common belief when anything happens that can't be easily justified: "it has been written." The belief was that one's fate is written at birth and the prophecy must be fulfilled. We have no control of that fate and nothing we do can alter the course of events. Unlike mine, his mother had tried to talk him out of the idea, but had finally given him her blessing seeing how determined Gjeto was. It was a big decision and a noble one for sure. Serve God and those in need; that was his mission. Regardless of faith, religion, or no religion, anyone who dedicates his life and service to a cause has embraced a noble decision and I applaud their courage. He left home and was sent to a boys-only school at the Illyricum College at the Franciscan Monastery in Shkodër. Gjeto was the second-born son of my maternal grandparents. His parents had plans for him to marry and work on the family farm one day, but he had other plans of his own. Living in a country and in an era of high illiteracy, his passion for education was very unusual. He had decided his entire life to serving others until the day he died in 1993.

Gjeto would come home and spend summers in Shënkoll, but most of the time when the other kids were playing and having fun, Gjeto had his head buried in his books. He would join the kids for short periods of time, but because he couldn't relate to any of them, he would go back to his books. None of the other kids in Shënkoll had had any education beyond the fourth grade and Gjeto had grown so far apart from them, having spent his entire life with some of the biggest brains of the Albanian educated class.

At the age of twelve, after completing basic studies in Shkodër, he was accepted at a college in Rome. During his college years, he made only one trip home during the summer of 1944. Even this summer was no different from the previous ones when he was in Shkodër, except that he was ever more of a stranger to everyone, including his family. After a couple of days catching up with his family, he went back to his routine of locking himself in his study room all day. He would only come out for supper or to take a short break. During his breaks, he would take a walk at the family vineyard, never without a book in his left hand and rosaries in his right.

In 1948 he would have completed his studies and would have been ordained Catholic priest. He was so close to achieving his dream. He had not seen his family in three years, so he decided to spend the summer break home, before he can get back to his last semester. He boarded a ship from Bari, Italy to Bar, Yugoslavia,[20] and from Yugoslavia he proceeded via land to home in Shënkoll. From Bar to his home, it is about one hundred kilometers. After a journey of three days, two at sea and one on the land, he made it home. He had left a young boy and was now a grown mature man.

---

[20] The names of these two cities (Bari and Bar) are coincidentally very similar, but are indeed two different cities in two different countries.

While enjoying his time with his family, the news broke of a dispute between Albanian's communist government and its Yugoslav counterpart, which lead to the immediate closing of all borders between Albania and Yugoslavia. No one was allowed in or out. Gjeto was unable to leave the country again, as his only way out had been through Yugoslavia. Many things had been happening in Albania during this time, where a war on religion, especially against Catholic clergy was in full swing. Most priests had been jailed or executed. The Franciscan monastery in Shkodër had been converted into a jailhouse. Most churches were closed and repurposed by the government. Some were simply demolished. The only gods worshipped were the communist leaders of the world with Enver Hoxha as the most revered prophet.

Gjeto was unable to get back to school and the government pressured him to get a job as schoolteacher in the small town of Vukël in the Kelmend mountains north of Albania. Vukël is where his ancestors had migrated from many years ago. For three years since his return from Rome, he spent his days teaching and his evenings studying, praying, and thinking of his uncertain future. Three weeks after his brother's escape, in November of 1951, he got the news. He knew he would not be safe either now and he had to do something about it. On the same day he got the news he decided to escape as well. Having spent last three years in the area, which was close to the border of Yugoslavia, he knew the terrain very well. Beyond the towns of Vukël and Selcë, the area was very remote far from everyone with no infrastructure or any connection to civilized word. The closest metropolitan city, Shkodër, was one day away in travel. People in the cities would say, *It was also far from God.* He had never fathomed spending his life teaching kids communist doctrine in the Alps of Albania when his dream was to follow the teaching of Jesus and profess the Catholic faith. Now that his brother was an escapee, his chances of continuing became even slimmer. He thought his plan through and chose to leave through a path that was so remote where there was no barbed electric fence, thus, a little easier to escape, but the natural conditions were worse than the fence. One thing was sure: wherever fence was not needed, it was deemed impossible for any human being to get through. The terrain is rigid and covered in snow most of the year and the cold would kill anything living. Only wild goats and some stubborn highlanders would ever think of living there. No one else in their right mind would. Gjeto seized the opportunity and when the time was right, he walked for many hours, maybe days, and made it to Yugoslavia. After two years in Yugoslavia, he managed to go to Italy again. He managed to finish his studies and was ordained a Catholic priest in 1955.

The Radi family had been labeled Të Prekun since Gjergj's escape, but having a Catholic priest now, was even worse. Having a Catholic priest and escapee at the same time, was a double jeopardy crime against the regime. Like the other Të Prekun families, they were deprived of good jobs, higher education, or any small privileges. The secret police were constantly watching every move of the family, trying to find something to further their persecution and possibly imprison someone else from the family. For the most part, knowing what they were dealing with, the family tried to conform with the rules established and accepted their fate. They worked hard and stayed out of trouble. In April of 1973, the regime got tired of waiting for the Radis to make a mistake and decided to make one up for them. An article was published in the state-controlled newspaper, *Zëri i Popullit*, which claimed that Gjeto Radi had published an article in the Italian Newspapers (not sure which) condemning the communist regime of Enver Hoxha. I don't know who thought that would be a good idea to come up with, but making sense didn't matter as long as they could make it stick. And so, it did stick and some bought the story. The local government of Shënkoll gathered and condemned publicly the letter and the family of the traitor. It was decided that this travesty can be only be paid by sending Gjergj's family to an internment camp, for a second time, so maybe this time they can learn a lesson. How Gjergj's wife and kids had anything to do with this story was never made clear to me nor anyone else, but that's what the Party decided and that's what they did. At this time, Gjergj's older son, Llesh, was married. In December of 1973, Gjergj's family—Prenë, Llesh with his wife Pashkë, and Pal were loaded into a military truck and sent to a remote town called Piraj in Lezhë district. This was not as far as Tepelenë, their previous camp, and it was not as bad as Tepelenë. The sentence was three years, during which they could not leave the town without permission—which was never granted. During this three-year internment period, Llesh was blessed with a boy who they named Marjan. While at the first internment in Tepelenë, they lost Vitore, at the second internment Marian was born. This family had seen it all by now. At the end of their three-year sentence, they were allowed to return home.

Every Sunday, the main Italian channel, RA1, broadcasts a mass from Saint Peter's Cathedral in Vatican City. Our old television could pick up the waves though with bad picture quality and with many interruptions. Most Sundays my mother would sit and watch the mass. I don't know how many laws she broke watching foreign channels and a mass, but I remember her looking for a brother she had not seen in about forty-years. She had last seen him when he was a teenager and now had to be in his late fifties. Gjeto Radi had been completely cut off from his family and no one had any idea of his whereabouts. They suspected he was in Italy, but that was all they knew. Sunday masses in Vatican City are a major event with hundreds of priests and thousands of people watching. Every time my mother watched that mass, she picked a different brother from the crowded priest pool in attendance. "This one looks like my father." "This one has my noose." "This one has my hair." "This one walks like my sister." I doubt her brother was even in the area in most of those occasions. He had been a parishioner in Rome somewhere but not at the Vatican. I can't tell you how many times she changed the brother prototype, but at least they were Catholic priests and we consider them all brothers. Until 1991 no one had any communication with Gjeto. He dedicated his life to Jesus and sacrificed everything for him. He lived in Rome and served in several parishes. In 1991 my brother, Gjergj, escaped to Italy and after a short time there he went on a quest to look for uncle Gjeto. At the time, my uncle's health had deteriorated and he was sent to a convalescent home in Palermo, Italy, to be taken care of. Gjeto died in 1993 and was buried in Palermo. Several years after, his remains were brought to Albania accompanied by a delegation from the Vatican and the funeral was broadcasted by Albanian national television, TVSH, now controlled by a Democratic government. His personal effects consisted of many diplomas, a bible, a rosary, and some philosophy and theology books in Italian, Latin, and Ancient Greek languages.

He is finally resting in his homeland in Albania.

XI.   My Mother

My mother, Marë Dedja, the youngest child of Dedë Zef Radi and Mri Dodja, was born in the village of Shënkoll, Lezhë, on March 23, 1934. Her family had a very similar history to my father's family. They came from same region of Kelmend and followed same paths migrating down to the Adriatic coastline around the same timeline as I have described earlier regarding my father's family path. My father's family belonged to the Selcë clan and my mother's to the Vukël clan. Both these clans are part of the Kelmend tribe and are considered brother clans. Marë was the youngest of five. She had two brothers: Gjergj and Gjeto, and two sisters: Tereze and File. Her mother died during childbirth together with the unborn child. Due to a poor healthcare system, women routinely died during childbirth. Childbirth death was so common that when a child was born, Albanians congratulated the mother first for having made it before congratulating the newborn. My mother was only eight years when her mother died. The loss of her mother was devastating, as it would be for an eight-year-old girl. Her father remarried and they had another son, Luigj. My mother was raised by her father and her stepmother, Marë Lekja, who "was as close to a mother as one can be," my mother would say. I too, remember my step-grandmother. I loved her and she loved all of us so much. I never met any of my grandparents, and she was the closest thing to a grandparent. I have always felt a vacuum in me because of the absence of my grandparents. I was only six when she died and I remember very little of her. Also, we didn't live close and didn't see each other much, but I do remember that she was a wonderful human being. God rest her soul.

My grandfather, Dedë Zef Radi, was a well-respected man in his community and beyond. My mother's common stories included her school years, where she excelled, and her trips to family and friends' homes, mostly the well-to-do. Her school years meant elementary school only: four years. Besides the family troubles, her childhood was a good one and she was happy. Happiness comes in many forms and the loss of her mother was not something that went away ever, but as the laws of nature dictate, the living must live.

Equality. This is what the Socialism-Communism doctrine was based on and tried to sell. In reality, it was anything but equality. There was some truth to that you can say. People were equally stripped of their property and human rights. A kilogram of sugar or salt was the same price everywhere, in every government store (those were the only ones). The meaning of equality, however, had been lost in translation. Equality in communist Albania didn't mean the same thing. We must update the dictionary to account for the form of equality that was portrayed in Albania between 1945 and 1992. What equality should mean is that people have equal opportunities and rights without prejudice, religion, age, gender, or other differences. Communists were the masters of discrimination and yet sold it as equality. Or I should say, they simply imposed it on their subjects, as people had no saying and had to obey. It was an appealing idea at first. Everyone likes to be free: free of foreign occupation and free to live under a local government of their choosing. With the exception of a short period of time between 1912 and 1939, Albania had been occupied and ruled by several foreign rulers. Some were better than others, but at the end of the day they had no business taking over the small country and rule it as they pleased just because it was weak and unable to defend itself—not for the lack of not trying though. The resentment of foreign powers had reached its peak with the German Nazi occupation. No one liked what came after, though, and they rebelled and tried and failed and then submitted. A systematic submission to the point of not being able to even dream out loud. Persecution was not a social class in its natural form against another, a race against another, or even a religious group against another. As a religious minority, I can attest to the fact that I have never felt to be in a minority based on religion, even though I was a Catholic in a country where Catholics accounted for only about twenty percent of the population.[21] I don't think anyone ever felt like they were in a minority on the basis of religious beliefs—not to mention the fact that all religions were banned between 1968 and 1990. The communist regime was finally exterminated only in 1992, but I use the year 1990 as the end of the ban on religion because it was in this year that, under international pressure, the clergy were freed from the political jails. No official announcement was made that it was okay to practice religion, but people took it upon themselves and most importantly, the brave clergy who had spent most of their lives in hard political prisons continued their mission undeterred.

There were other types of classes created and put one against the other in the ugliest possible way. One of the most heinous reform communists professed was the "Lufta e Klasave," the war of classes. Who were these classes that were supposed to be fighting each other? As far as communists admitted, it was the proletariat against the capitalist. Depending on the day of the week there were so many synonyms used to describe the prosecuted class that it's hard to keep up: capitalist, bourgeois,[22]

---

[21] There are no real statistics that I am aware of about the population based on religion. These are estimates based on other studies and best effort by the author. A true census counting has not been made in recent times.

[22] According to *Webster's Dictionary*, the term refers to someone belonging to middle-class. According to Marxist Doctrine, this was a reference to the ruling class who owned most of the wealth. The term was used as a synonym to aristocracy.

fascist, Nazis, kulak, enemy of the people, and so many more. But the essence was all the same: the pros and cons of the communist regime. In the communist playbook, this was pure good versus evil. Anyone who had possessed any wealth or education or had held any position in any pre-communist era was classified as bourgeois. Trouble was, a low-level official could decide with the strike of a pen if one was a sinner or a saint—proletariat or bourgeois. It is almost ironic that the whole drama with these so-called bourgeois class labels was played when most officials at the time were uneducated and had very little to no knowledge of the terminology they had grown so accustomed to using.

It was also pathetic to call someone bourgeois simply because they owned a small piece of land that in a real aristocratic class wouldn't have been enough to build the servants' quarters. Yet these uneducated people, who blindly took anything the Marxist doctrine had professed and implemented, had the power to sign orders they couldn't even read or understand. Some of these people were pure illiterates who couldn't even sign their names and instead simply dipped their thumb in paint and signed using their thumb prints (Albania seems to have been the pioneer of biometrics before anyone was even talking about it). Of course, certain individuals from a deserved bourgeois class managed to be relabeled proletariat if they contributed a little to the regime by ratting on their fellow bourgeois or anyone else deemed of interest to the Party. Communists and their supporters thus were good. Everyone else was evil. But how about the other classes of "Klasa Punetore" (working class) and "Fshatarësia Kooperativiste" (collective farming people)? The first referred to everyone living in metropolitan areas and cities, and the second referred to people living in Kooperativë or villages. City people were the new bourgeois and the village people were referred to as "Fshatar" a derogatory term meaning, or at least equivalent to, peasant. Naturally, then, peasants were people of no culture or intellect in the views portrayed by the elite. These were people of no value. Whoever was born in a village had to die there unless some miracle worked its way and one managed to marry someone from a city. People in cities worked in much better conditions after manufacturing and other production plants established. They also had any and all government jobs in every big and small town from teachers, doctors, and more. They got paid more, and work wasn't as hard as working in the fields. They also had better food and supplies. Their stores sold the best bread when the ones producing the wheat, Fshatars, on the other hand, ate the nasty corn bread. It was not their fault but bad luck that they were born in cities. Now, this is of course only for comparison, but people in cities were also prosecuted. Their homes, stores, manufacturing plants, and everything else that made the cities breathe were sequestered and became government property where the previous owners were forced to work for a salary decided by the government. It was the war of classes that turned everyone against one another. And for what? Resources, opportunities, and recognition: anything of value. By turning people against each other, it was easier for the elite to control everyone.

What about women? If you heard the propaganda machine and the government-controlled media, television, radio, or newspapers, women had the greatest equality unparalleled with any country in the world. Sure, the government had ensured that at least on paper, women would not be discriminated against. There were several women who held very high-level government positions and some women had similar jobs like men. On the surface all seemed wonderful. But a country's laws are only as good as their enforcement. If you believed everything that was said, women from the most democratic societies of the West would have wanted to live in Albania. How far from the truth was the lie sold by the regime propaganda? Part of the inequality was a result of centuries-old practices of this patriarchal society, which reached its peak under Ottoman Islamic rule and its 500-year reign. Part of it was the fact that the elite was not interested in equality. They were interested in control. The more people were controlled downstream, the easier their job was at the top. The war of classes ensured one class was kept down by the other class. And all the elite had to do is keep the top under control. Women, then, were kept under the control of men. That took care of half of the population.

My mother, like most women, was no different in this climate. She was born in a well-to-do family with land and property. This was before communist rule, but very patriarchal. They had people working for them and most family members enjoyed their life in abundance. The men ran the family business and the women took care of the household affairs. Boys went hunting and playing cards and girls assisted with household duties. Not to confuse this with the high society of Europe, but their life was somewhat better than most. They had owned lots of fertile land and that earned them a good living. They went to church every Sunday and prayed before dinner every night. Religion was an important aspect of their life.

The establishment of communist rule spared no one with anything of value: intellect, possessions, wealth, land, or anything that was of value to the new government. It was not enough to take everything from people, but people were also persecuted for having ever owned anything. I can't tell why this would constitute a crime, but the communists never ceased to amaze. Their justification was that the wealth was created by taking advantage of others. The righteous police in action.

When the churches were destroyed, in the campaign of 1968, when Albania was declared the only atheist country in the world, and all religious symbols with them, including the church bell of the town of Shënkoll where my mother is from, disappeared. No one knew its fate until 1990, when my mother's stepbrother Luigj Radi and her cousin Shtjefen Radi had brought it back to its rightful place: the church. They had hidden it for twenty-two years while risking being imprisoned (or worse) in a clear act of courage and defiance. This is where my mother came from and some of that was cultivated in us. Love for God, country, and family.

XII.   A New Era

When my father received a fifteen-year sentence, he wrote a letter to his fiancée, my mother. Although they were not in love, as one might think of love, since this was an arranged engagement and they had probably not even exchanged a word with each other yet, writing such letter had been devastating for my father. Calling off an engagement, especially when there was nothing between the couple, but some other circumstances called for, was never easy. Doing so meant admitting the end of his life and the acceptance of his fate in slavery. Nonetheless, my father saw it right to do his noble duty and not let his fiancée's life go wasted shedding tears for a man she never met rotting in jail. He had decided that it was the right thing to do to let her go. He began to write saying how much he had been looking forward to spend the rest of his life with her, but time was not in their favor and that he didn't think it was meant for them to be together.

"One life wasted is one too many," he said, "but yours doesn't have to be wasted too." He gave her his blessing, thus, to break the engagement and marry someone else.

"You should not have to suffer because of me. Live your life and forget about me," he wrote. "It would be best for us both."

Her whole family was gathered while she read loudly to everyone. Everyone started crying profusely. My mother read the letter in front of her family. It would have been improper for him to write to her and most definitely for her to read it out loud under normal circumstances, but these circumstances were not normal. This is not a decision that is easily made ever, but at that time and place it was even harder. People didn't just break engagements, not even if someone is sent to jail. This was a time when "until death do us apart" really meant what it said. Even though vows are exchanged at marriage, for them it really began at the engagement. The promise was made and promises are kept. There was also the "being in the same boat" thing. Both these families and most honest Albanians were fighting Communism. Standing by each other now meant more than ever. I'm not sure what must have been going through my father's mind, but it was not very common for anyone to take that step, to tell his fiancée to move on! He was sent to prison mainly for his brother's doings yet he doesn't want anyone to suffer for him. Sure, he had done his part, or was planning to, but still he wasn't a criminal. He was a hero in my book. Anyone who stands up for family and country and freedom is a hero. Noble, indeed.

On the other hand, my mother now had a choice to make: Wait for an uncertain future, or try her luck elsewhere. What could she do? Who would respect her if she left him? Maybe some would understand, but... She picks the first. She had already made her choice, but as it was customary, she had to ask her father for his blessing first. There wasn't anyone without tears while the words came out of her trembling lips shaking like someone in the middle of an ice storm. She could barely get to the bottom of the letter, where a simply one-word sentence closed the later. Goodbye. She skipped that one.

A couple of days went by, and as instructed by her father some members of her family had planned a trip to visit him in jail. Along with some clothes and food, a letter had to be delivered to him. Although he had written his letter, deep down he was expecting a rejection of his proposal. He didn't want it, but he had to do it. He had hoped this would be her first act of defiance. This was an important letter that sealed the fate of my parents.

"Dear husband," she began to write. Women didn't call their husbands by their name but addressed them as husband or something else.

"I pray to God this letter finds you well. I pray one day we will both look at this and be proud of the choices we are making here today because this is the right choice. My fate and yours are one, and I am not leaving you ever while you still breathe."

"You need never ask me again this question, because the answer will not change. I have made the choice once the day my father promised me to you. If we want to fight this evil that has usurped our country, we must stick together. And together we will stay. This is not just about you and me anymore. It is about our two families united. It is about a partner in struggle and hope soon in life," she continued.

She concluded the letter: "Please take care of yourself and don't worry about me. I am all right with my family and will be fine. We will be together soon."

In my father's darkest day, when he thought his life was eventually over, but it was a matter of time, he wasn't thinking about himself but his future wife and how he didn't want her life to be ruined because of him. On the other hand, when my mother's dreams of a girl planning for a wedding were cut short, she didn't think of herself but of the promise she had made and how she intended to keep that promise until death do them apart even though vows were not exchanged yet. These simple people with simple lives were put to a great test of courage and selflessness and they excelled. I'm glad this happened, or I would not be writing here today. Of course, this was not a single case of courage and loyalty of my parents. This was just one of the many brave men and women who sacrificed for each other. I'm sure such a decision by my mother helped my father get through his prison years that seemed to be eternal.

When everything seemed to be lost after my father's imprisonment and a long sentence handed to him, very little hope of anything bright to come was seen possible from either of my parents. Years went by very slowly. Many things changed. My mother's family was stripped of all their property like everyone else—except that they were wealthy before, and her brothers left the country. Her family and my fathers' family started looking more alike. In fact everyone in Albania was looking alike now. Socialism means all are equal, except that equal means "all equally stripped of anything they possess." In 1961, my father was released from jail and came home. Before he could take some time to relax, he had to immediately start taking over the family affairs. His brother Nikë's health had deteriorated a lot and he was the only man in the family able to provide for the rest of them.

Nikë died shortly after the wedding, from an undiagnosed disease at age forty-five. He had held the fort while being severely ill. Coincidentally, Nikë's father had also died at the same age. I think it was very simple: overwork, bad nutrition, and the physical consequences of being oppressed and depressed. That would do it. He left behind his young wife and four kids. His wife was also pregnant with his fifth child, Pashkë. She was born five months after her father's death.

My father had wasted many years in jail and now, although not really in a position to get married, he wanted to make right by my mother and not let her wait any longer. She had held her side of the bargain and it was time for Zef to hold his. The big wedding of their dreams was out of the question, but they had to marry, nonetheless. Quickly they made arrangements and had the long-awaited wedding. These families had a lot to celebrate: Zef's release and marriage. The newly married couple started their lives together under hardships of all kinds. Nikë's passing, was very devastating. Seems this family can never get a break. The couple had eight kids eventually: four boys and four girls. I happened to be the youngest: a blessing in many cultures, but a curse in my case. It was very common to have many kids at the time, although eight was a little more than usual. Time is proving that it wasn't such a bad idea, based on many nations' experience of aging and shrinking populations. Mathematics is simple: more kids mean more demands, and when the resources are limited, it means everyone suffers more. During the time when they owned farms, this also meant more people to work the farm. Now the farms were gone, but old habits die hard.

3. A Son is Born

Many times, I asked, why!

Why was I not born in a different era or in a different country? Why am I not a little taller or have better hair? So many unanswered whys. I wish I never grew up, sometimes, and had never learned the things I know. It was much easier not to think of things like country, duty, and other grown-up stuff. Children are blessed in many respects. Everything is provided for them (not in my case, but still easier); magical things appear on the table or in their rooms. Wouldn't it be great to be able to do that when you are grown up as well!

Why do people kill other people? Why are people crueler than most species when they possess a superior level of intelligence? Why do most people suffer for food when the whole world has more than it needs to feed its population? Ah, I wish I knew. Who knows? One thing I do know, though, is that it can be a lot easier. It is doable. I used to observe the birds in the nest at the entrance of our house. Swallow birds liked to build their nest around the light bulb of the entrance of our house; it's where they hatch their eggs and raise their babies. Five or six of them and somehow the mother made sure they all had equal amount of food, and plenty of it too. A bird with no hands, legs, or speech or other functions we humans are blessed with manages it. Why can't we? Others have done superb jobs studying human behavior, so I will let you find the answers for yourself, but after all being a human is not that bad. It is the ability to observe and judge that makes us interesting.

I wished I was born in a different country in a different era and I had the perfect prototype: Middle Ages Europe. England maybe. I was fascinated by the acceptance of fate these people had. No one asked why a king is the king and believed God appointed him. It was easy. The king says so, because he is the son of God, much similar to Jesus or other prophets. But then daydreaming was over and reality kicked in. My mother calls me to do a chore or go eat or something else that interrupts my dream. I return to 1980s in no time. We all ask why and we do it frequently. I asked why being the youngest in the family is a curse, even though everyone in the family tells me it isn't so. Being the youngest is like being the last person standing on the tarmac when boarding a plane with limited seating and you have a standby ticket. Being the youngest is like being the only kid at a summer camp who can't swim. Being the youngest is like a bird with no feathers to fly. It hurts and it hurts a lot. Why is it my fault that kids are born at a specific order and someone has to be the last? Why am I less important to my parents than my older siblings? When we think of the communist regime and the tough times, we fail to mention the part of the problem we were:

all of us. We failed to address centuries old practices that derived from a feudal, hierarchical, patriarchal, rotten system that kept much of the world in the dark ages and still does so in many parts today. The older son gets it all; others get nothing even though there wasn't much to share. As if others don't count. Who, ever came up with that method? We talk about persecution from the totalitarian communist government, but how about persecution from the totalitarian parents? Who told them they could decide for us all the time? Because they gave birth to us! Someone had to. Ah, this is too complicated, so I better stop here.

Even in the worst of times, the birth of a child calls for celebration. A new life. A new hope. A new promise. The cycle of life. Births of children, even in this poor family of mine, for the most part were marked by celebrations. The evening of December 16, 1976, was not exactly something I would call an extremely happy evening, the kind of an evening you would expect under the circumstance when a boy is born in a highly patriarchal society. So deep was the difference between having a boy versus a girl that when a boy was born, people said, "me jete të gjatë djalin," long live the boy. When a girl was born, people said, "mos u mërzit," don't despair. If a couple had many girls in a row with no boys and another girl was born, that would be almost like a funeral with people literally crying to the news of another girl. God! How cruel were these people! For the record, there were and still are deep differences by region, social class, and demographics when it comes to embracing this medieval tradition. Not everyone subscribed to this cruelty then nor now.

Yes, a boy was born and that would have been a cause for celebration, but this was the fourth now, and the eighth child of the poor couple from a small village of Mali i Jushit in the rural areas of Shkodër. The news reached the family the next day, due to lack of communication means, even though the maternitet was only three kilometers away in the town center of Barbullush. Maternitet was only for childbirth. It was not a true hospital in the literal sense of the word. The exhausting mother gave life to a healthy boy, exact weight unknown since no one kept records of that, but pretty normal based on the mami's assessments. Most kids at the time were born at home assisted by an experienced old woman, or many, or if possible a midwife, but this boy was lucky to have been born at a clinic, something fairly new at the time and place. The clinic consisted of a couple of experienced midwifes that were called *mami*, not to be confused with the word *mami*, which is a nickname for mother. *Mami* meant someone experienced in delivering babies and had some medical training to be able to administer an injection. In Albanian, the word *mami* means both things, so context matters.

There wasn't any medical equipment for anything other than for assisting in the birth: not much different than being born at home. There were few beds with old blankets and gray sheets. The only source of heat was a very small wooden stove at one corner that barely produced enough heat to make a coffee. The mother went to the clinic accompanied by her sister-in-law. They walked in the cold of December on a muddy country road because there were no means of transportation at all. No men would go with her, not even the husband, as it was considered taboo for a man to be present while the woman is giving birth.

This is a historically Christian family, but some of these customs are more adequate to a Muslim family. Why then does a Christian family resemble a Muslim family? Albania had been under the Ottoman Islamic rule for about 500 years and an unknown number of people—some believe roughly sixty percent or more of the population—was converted to Islam. The ones who didn't convert have so much in common with the ones who did that it is hard to tell them apart. To add to this confusion, we have a country, Albania, which was once declared as the only atheist country in the world, with an Islamic majority with a strong Christian past—and with people ostensibly practicing neither. Culturally speaking though, the Islamic laws installed by Ottoman Empire were very much the norm. For twenty-two years the government persecuted anyone who practiced any religion. Before the Ottoman occupation, all of Albania practiced Christianity—and Paganism before that. But at the time, the majority of the population still lived as if it were still the Dark Ages.

Mother and son came home, eventually, after three days at the clinic. Mother was happy to get it over with and the son was happy to be free, or so he thought. He had no idea that the mother's womb, as confined as it was, would be the closest thing to freedom he would have for a very long time. Little did he know the cruel world he was coming into, a world filled with poverty, torture, killings, imprisonments, internments, absolute lack of freedom, and access to anything vital. Little did he know that this wasn't the world he had been looking forward to see. Had he known that, he would have tried to stay in the womb for as long as possible. It was warm there. At least no one bothered him. But it was too late now. He is here to stay and that cannot be reversed.

The son was named "Nosh." That son was me.

I.   Childhood

Here is where I begin my journey to the beautiful life in the golden era of Albanian Communism. Here is where all the dreams mentioned by the propaganda would come true. There was a catch, though. Those dreams were only for the few on top and I had been assigned to the other side, without my asking. I was an "enemy of the people" from birth.

They say don't judge a book by its cover, but the picture on the cover of this book (original picture above) is me six years old with my mother. It was the very first picture I had taken because there were no cameras and taking a picture was quite a treat. The day was an interesting day of mixed feelings. Sadness, happiness, and anxiety. It was the summer of 1983. Summers in that part of the world are very hot. It doesn't rain for many months at the time and temperatures reach 35–40 degrees Celsius. My father was admitted at the regional hospital in the big city of Shkodër I had never seen. My mother took me to visit him: she took each child one at the time and finally that day was my turn. When she told me she was going to take me to see the city, I didn't sleep for days until the day came. God forgive me, but I was more excited about seeing the city of Shkodër than seeing my father. Dad had to get a procedure done, which consisted of removing some dead veins from a previous surgery he had had years prior, a residue from either his military, internment camp, or jail years, or all combined; none of this was life threatening. The healthcare system in Albania was so primitive that anything could kill you. In any event, he did spend a month at the hospital and at the end all went well. They also say a picture is worth a thousand words. If you examine this picture closely, although it is hard to see all the details—but in my mind they are still fresh—you see that my clothes are a combination of heavy winter and hot summer clothes. My pants aren't even mine; they're rolled at the bottom several times because they are much longer: winter pants made of thick fabric. I don't recall who they belonged to (an older sibling maybe?), but they weren't mine, that's for certain. You can't see it in the photo, but there's a belt tightened so hard around my small waste to keep the pants in place because the waist size was about ten sizes wider than my tiny waist. The sweater is a short-sleeved sweater, but it's made of wool. That was mine. It was hand-knitted by one of my sisters. Yes, it was hot, but I didn't mind it. The sweater looked good at least, and heat was a small price I paid for looking fashionable. The shoes were either borrowed from a friend or a sibling. Borrowing clothes from a friend was normal, for special occasions, and this was a very special occasion for me. Even though the picture is in black and white, the original colors were pretty dark too and not much different from the picture. Most clothes at the time were dark. This photo would be typical for an American Western, or maybe something you'd see at World War I or World War II museum but not in 1983 Europe! That was one of the best days of my early life, dad aside, and that picture is definitely worth a thousand words.

The most precious carefree happy time of one's life should be the childhood. This is when a child is taken care of, caressed, provided for, and the only thing the child should be thinking about is playing and having fun. My childhood, if one can call it such, was far from what a childhood should be. My toys were tools for working in the fields or some other kind. My camping days were spent in the fields of tobacco gathering leaves during the hottest summer days or gathering medicinal herbs that school assigned us for summer, but there was always something to do other than having a little bit of fun. My vacations were days at home helping with daily chores. Today I occasionally enjoy a cigar and it always reminds me of those days of gathering the goddamn leaves, putting them on a goddamn string, and hanging them on the goddamn wall to dry. The supervisor would come at the end of the day and examine the strings to make sure the leaves were tight on them, but not too tight and then sign our worksheet and let us go.

The workday was over, but the trouble was not. When we went home, we had to clean up ourselves from the grease the fresh tobacco leaves leave on your skin and the heavy smell of nicotine. Tobacco plants grow as high as eight feet tall. The leaves are large and so greasy that if you touch the leaves, you need to spend a significant amount of time to get rid of it. The process of removing that grease from your skin by scrubbing with dirt and then finishing up with soap was a huge undertaking. Soap was in short supply, so we couldn't afford to use any for the entire cleaning process: we used dirt to remove the bulk of the grease and only then did we finished with soap. Soap was this block of greasy matter that smelled horrible and looked nasty. Even that was in short supply and the "Nena Parti," the mother party, provided one bar of soap a month and for a high price. Showers were non-existent. There was no plumbing or running water at all, so we had to first warm the water and put it in a big bucket and wash ourselves by pouring water with a cup. The work with tobacco was in summer, so most of the time we didn't even heat the water. It made it harder to scrub the grease, but that was a choice we made between spending more time scrubbing or dealing with heating the water. On the weekends, we did manage to heat the water and washed a little better. This was the same process for taking baths as well for the winter and the summer. In the summer, we used the sun to warm the water for bathing. Who knew Albania was a pioneer in solar power! No solar panels needed. Just fill the bucket with water and place it in a sunny spot in the hottest time of the day and leave it there for hours. It warms up enough not to be cold, but not enough to remove the dirt. There were three of us from my family who worked on this tobacco endeavor at this time: my sister, my brother, and me. Because we worked together we had to take turns having only one bucket available. It may be hard to believe, but I was eight years old when I first became an expert harvester of tobacco—and this was just one of many jobs I worked at as a child.

At the age of almost seven, I started school. I couldn't wait to go to school. I had missed the previous year because my birthday is in December and school starts in September. The summer seemed much longer the year preceding the start of school and if it had been one day longer, I would have fainted. I finally had new clothes, maybe for the first time in my life—as far as I can remember—and a school bag, not a new one of course, but a bag nonetheless. Being the youngest of eight, I had to use a bag that was previously used by my other siblings. Perhaps it was passed down three or four times or more from one sibling to the other by the time it became mine. Each one had to make sure to take good care of it so it could be reused by the next child and then the next as many times as possible. Despite that, I had to patch it and stich it in many places so that my books wouldn't fall out of the huge holes. At some point there were more patches than the original fabric on that bag. I remember that bag vividly. It was black fake leather with two handles and closed with a buckle half way down. Besides the buckle that still worked, surprisingly, after so many years, the rest of the bag was all worn out. Its shape had changed so much that you couldn't tell what the original shape was. I did get a new pen, though, the cost of which was 175 lekë (the Albanian currency), the equivalent of probably two thousand American dollars in the year of 2021. You better believe when I tell you that I slept with that pen under my pillow for a long time. I had nightmares of someone taking it away from me and woke up screaming and crying. I checked on it several times a day to make sure it was still there, well hidden under my pillow, mattress, or my special hiding spot in the small shoebox I had for my books. That box was the only thing I had available for my school, besides the bag. Both the box and the bag were usually stowed under the bed. Homework and studying were done by placing my bag on my knees and the books on top, using the bag as a table. Reading was fine, but writing and drawing in that position was hard. Sometimes I was able to use the dinner table, but that multipurpose table was always busy with something: another sibling studying, mother cooking, or a sister making some king of clothing. I even remember the brand of that pen. It was called "Senator." I have no idea where it came from. It was way too nice to have been made in Albania because there was no way Albania could make such a thing. All of Albania's import at the time came from some other communist country, so "Senator" didn't seem to make sense, but who knows? I do know, though, that it was black, fat, and it felt good to own one of them. I swear, I don't know what made my parents buy me one of those, but it was like buying a Ferrari or a yacht today. It was a very big deal. I guess one day I will give up trying to figure it out and just live with the memory that this pen was probably the best thing that ever happened to me for a very long time in my childhood.

I was a very good student. I had a great love for knowledge. It came naturally. I also loved to succeed and exceed. I was determined not to be last. I loved to be first and *had* to be first. For a long time, I didn't understand most of what was going on, and being told you are from a Të Prekun family was almost like saying you are Albanian. It didn't bother me. I didn't know better. I thought that was normal. As far as I was concerned, I didn't see my family as cowards but as heroes, so the label given by someone who had never contributed anything to anyone besides themselves didn't irritate me. By contrast, it gave me some pride that my family didn't become communist puppets, spies, or rats. Instead, they stood up to the regime. Toward the end of the first grade, I was given a trophy for being the best student in my class. I hit a straight 100% record. The trophy had to match the record, so instead of anything from an Albanian hero, I was a given a pin to wear on my chest with the head of Mao Tse-tung, the Chinese dictator. What an honor!

After school, I had to do many chores, other than study, and that left me with little time to play. I loved to play the games where partisans (freedom fighters) fought the Germans. This was the influence of Albanian-made movies of propaganda, which showed how Albanian partisans fought off the mighty Nazi army. They always showed the other guerrillas, such as Ballists, as the enemy, so we didn't like them either as kids. Little did I know that Ballists were the real patriots. A country of 2.5 million people had been so strong, according to these movies, that we made Nazi Germany tremble at the sound of Albania.

I didn't have any toys, but I did have a wooden gun, which I built with whatever I could gather around. It was made with three pieces of wood and the finished product was an "F" shape. It looked nothing like a gun nor a toy gun, but my imagination was so wild that to me it looked like a German machine gun from the World War II Albanian movies. To be fair, the real gun looks very plain too: one long tube with one handle and one skinny long magazine that also serves as the second handle. Quite plain, as you can imagine. I think the gun in question is a model MP40, but at that time I simply knew that every Albanian movie about World War II had one. It was easily recognizable as the German machine gun. Many partisans had those too, because they had taken them from the Germans they killed or captured. It was not that hard to mimic it and my wooden gun just did the job.

Now, my friend Aleks, on the other hand, had a real aluminum pistol that I would borrow from him from time to time. Aleks was the only son of the family (with three sisters) and he was treated somewhat like a prince, under the circumstances. Although in despair, Albania continued to be a patriarchal society and the boys were still treated better than girls. Being the only boy in the family was considered a jewel. There is a special word in Albanian for only sons: "Djalë Dëshiri," which means "Son of Dreams," something long waited for, that finally came true. His family was smaller than mine; his parents had better jobs and made more money, so they could afford a real toy. Furthermore, they were not on the wrong side of the regime, so it made a difference. They were neither pro nor against the regime, at least officially, even though they didn't like the regime more than my family did. They were what would be the majority of Albanian citizens. His father operated a Kooperativë tractor for living and earned a good salary compared to the ones who did the manual labor. Even Aleks didn't have much else, though, but he had more new clothes.

I was very good at this game of partisans fighting Germans. I always played the partisan, since Germans were the bad guys and I could convince my friends to let me be the partisan: a commander of partisans most of the time. Somehow, I had this persuasive nature and my friends did listen to me. You can say I was the unelected leader of my group of friends. As a kid, this was very appealing. Who doesn't like to be a hero of his country? Being the partisan commander was to us like being Superman or Spiderman is to today's kids. Sometimes I feel that I may have been a little unjust to my friends, but they must have forgiven me. I meant no harm. We were a group of four best friends who lived close and grew up together, and I was the only one who was a good student. They were mediocre but didn't really excel. I was always at the top of my class, in fact, but that would matter little since I wouldn't have been allowed to pursue any education. I was class president due to my impeccable academic record for many years, and that may have influenced my friends out of school too. As I got older, past fifth grade, the privilege of being class president was revoked too. The school principal was upset that it had gone that long unnoticed and the teacher of my class was criticized for allowing it to happen. Whatever the case with my friends may have been, that is how it went down. I loved them all dearly and they loved me very much. Isn't that how best friends are supposed to be anyways? I do think so!

The Communist government owned and controlled everything and no one was allowed to own anything. All property was confiscated. In cities, all businesses were nationalized, and in towns all land was collectivized. First the collectivization started as a voluntary measure, but of course the ones who didn't comply paid a very high price, some with their life. Also, in cases where someone very stubborn resisted, the government imposed very high taxes that were impossible, and as a result those who were stubborn gave up and joined the others.

Most things communists imposed on people to do were called *volunteering*. For instance, people were sent to work for free on major projects such as building railroads, and they were volunteers. Most major projects in the country, from building railroads to draining swamps, was done with slave labor (prisoners and internees) and/or with "volunteer" work. Some of the volunteer work was done on weekends and other times these volunteer campaigns were two weeks to one-month long undertakings. My family lived in a small village in the countryside, but the property was reduced to 1000 square meters. That was the allowed property for a given family, regardless of its size. You know who the real bourgeois were? The government. The government was the only owner and employer in the entire country. The rest was taken away and nothing new was allowed to be added. Workers were only allowed to own their working tools. In fact, they had to provide their own working tools, which consisted of farming primitive tools, such as shovels and picks. They had to take good care of the tools, because replacement was hard, not only because they were hard to be found in the only stores owned by—you guessed it, the government—but also, they were very expensive.

Everyone had to work for the new boss, The Government. Owning a car was forbidden, even though no one knew how much one would cost. They simply did not exist. Roads were deserted and only once in a while a government vehicle passed by. Owning household items such as television, refrigerator, or even a bicycle, was done with a special permission by the government. My family would never be approved one because of our background.

A Kooperativë was a large organization that consisted of one or many small villages, depending on the size of the village, and all residents from the age of fourteen, unless they went to high school, were required to register and become part of the workforce. Most skipped high school because the family needed the income. Some did it because they saw no point in going to high school. And mostly all did it for both reasons. The lucky ones who went to high school did it in part to skip work in a Kooperativë. And a very few did it for the sole purpose of education. Working was mandatory. Each town had one small general store where they sold groceries, clothes, and pretty much everything necessary. There was a separate store that sold bread and milk and vegetables and once in a while meat—more like bones with a little meat on them. These two stores supplied the whole village with everything, except that they had nothing.

In 1985 we purchased a second-hand television from an acquaintance who was selling it to buy a new one. Buying a television was another complex process. There was a very limited supply of television sets, all made in Albania and bad quality. If you wanted to buy one of those sets, you had to apply for and be approved by the government first. It was like applying for a firearm permit. My family would never get one because we were Të Prekun, so we didn't even bother apply. The price of this big box that showed communist propaganda most of the time, and some movies or documentaries here and there, came with a heavy price tag equivalent to one worker's yearly salary or more. Most families couldn't afford one, even if the approval was granted. Before we purchased ours, there were only three others in the whole area. The day the television came home, it was a celebration. Relatives and friends came to congratulate us like a special occasion, such as the birth of a child. We placed it on top of a wooden table in the largest room of the house, usually used as guest room. My sisters had made a special cover for that table. The only channel available was TVSH, the Albanian state station. The programs started at 6:00 P.M. and ended at 10:30 P.M. on weekdays, and on Sunday the programs started at 10:00 A.M. There was a kids' show first, usually some cartoons or movie, followed by weather and news and then a documentary of propaganda. Let's not forget that everything was propaganda.

Movies were full of propaganda. Kids shows were full of propaganda. News was propaganda. The only thing that was somewhat pure was sports. Every night the TV room, as we called it now, was full with neighbors coming to watch.

I am not sure why someone who calls himself a leader, someone responsible for the citizens of his country, would want his people to starve. I do understand that some countries simply have limited resources, but when a country like Albania has the resources and its government elects to starve its people, that is beyond my comprehension. It can be seemed almost like an experiment performed by Nazis during World War II. At least their goals were to find cures for some deceases, but Albanian communists did it to suppress their population further. Because the government was the sole owner and supplier of all goods, everything was in short supply and food was no different. Starvation. As long as I can remember, until 1992, after the fall of Communism, we never had enough food. I always went hungry. The majority of the population were constantly hungry, while those at the top had plenty and even managed to waste. I don't know who first said "money doesn't bring happiness," but not having anything sure brings misery. I can attest to that. Even if you had plenty of money—this was impossible—you couldn't buy anything because everything was rationed and the stores were empty. I guess here the theory holds some truth, when money possession doesn't help either. How could anyone have any money, when the government decided everyone's pay? It sure wasn't enough to get anything other than what the store provided.

Let me start with the bread, the most basic ingredient of an Albanian diet. Because there was very little of any food, bread had become even more important than ever. Bread was scarce and every person was entitled to a small ration of bread per day. Most of the time I remember, it was 800 grams, but sometimes it was reduced because the corn or wheat that was used to make the bread was needed to feed the livestock. Good prioritization: put an animal over a person. There was no extra even if you had lots of money to pay for it. The government set all the prices and they were very high. A loaf of wheat bread was priced forty lekë. A day's pay for a worker in the Kooperativë ranged from 30 lekë to 175 lekë, depending on where you worked. If you were in the lower bracket, you had to work an entire day and not be able to afford a load of bread. The rates were based on the productivity of your Kooperativë, which really depended on the fertility of the land and the availability or irrigation and other natural factors. For the same job two people on two different Kooperativës got paid different salaries. Prices, however, were all the same across the country. Our Kooperativë was ranked the second in the whole country on productivity. Our lands are very fertile and we, as a Kooperativë, even with the very poor technology, produced enough to feed a large portion of the country. Of course, most of it went to China to buy Chinese weapons, such as tanks, guns, and ammunition. After joining NATO in 2007, Albania had to pay to get rid of them. That's how useful they were.

Only during the summer months could we get wheat bread. For another three or four months, spring and fall, it was a mixed three parts corn and one part wheat. And during winter, it was all corn bread. Despite the fact that we, in our Kooperativë, produced enough wheat to feed half of the country, we ate mostly corn bread. During the months when we were given three parts corn bread and one part wheat, my mother had to surgically distribute the wheat bread among us in the fairest way possible. The ones who worked at the Kooperativë and needed to get lunch, got most of the wheat bread, and the rest of us—me and my brother, who didn't work yet in the Kooperativë—were served corn bread only. My mother too ate whatever was left, which meant nothing many days. One of the moments I looked forward to all day was the time when people returned from their long workdays. You know why? Because my siblings had saved a bite of wheat bread for my brother and me. I treated that bite of wheat bread as if it were a chocolate from the finest chocolatiers of Belgium. Sometimes I couldn't wait and just ate it right away; other times I saved it until dinner to eat is as a kind of dessert. Who would have thought that bread would be such a delicacy!

I have finally come to terms with corn bread. I like it so much now that whenever I'm down south, I ask for it, as corn bread is famous in the American south. I am sure that back in the days of slavery corn bread must have had a very similar tale as mine. Now the southern corn bread is so refined that I like it, although for a long time I resisted it. Much of my reluctance had to do with the fact that eating Albanian corn bread was like eating yellow rubber. This bread was so hard to chew and often the corn seeds were not even ground. Mice and other non-edible items were routinely found inside the bread. By the time it reached our table, it had been through all the stages of refining to make it inedible, that you had to develop special skills to be able to eat it. People got sick constantly and some died from dysentery and other diseases, some maybe even unknown to modern medicine since they only happened in this time and place. Who kept count of them? Just another day in paradise.

I have a special relationship with milk. No matter what it does to me, I can't ever get mad at it. My love for milk is unconditional. It breaks my heart still today after so many years of abundance of milk, when I have to dump some old spoiled milk. It is a king of precious material that has no real value in the market, but to me it is dear. This attachment to milk is the result of my growing up without enough of it because milk was another item that was rationed. My family of ten was entitled to about a liter of milk per day. If we were to drink American coffee with milk, but American coffee is not used in Albania, wouldn't have been enough milk for everyone's coffee. Not only was the amount so little, it wasn't even milk. By the time it reached my cup, it was less than half milk and the rest was mostly water. Before consuming the milk, my mother had to filter it through a fine net to keep the flies and other non-edible items out. That process of course reduced the size considerably and the more stuff was filtered, the more I grew anxious of having less milk left for me. I looked at the net getting fuller and the milk container getting smaller with anxiety. I wanted to stop my mother from letting certain items get away from the milk, so not to lose my ration. I stared at that milk with such admiration as if it were my first time seeing the Mona Lisa at the Louvre. Of course, the net kept large items out, but the dust and other small particles that were constantly part of the milk made it in anyway. Bacteria were probably having a field day. Thank God we boiled the milk and I guess most of the bacteria got killed, or our bodies became immune to them over time, but I still don't believe how we didn't all die from it. It could also be that we had so little that even if it was all germs, it was not enough to infect us. It's like using snake venom to cure a disease: if taken in small doses it can cure you, but if taken in large doses it kills you. There's a reason for everything, I guess. After all, the government must have been looking out for our welfare and made sure we took only small doses. I have spent fourteen years of my life waiting for a day when I could have enough milk. That day came only when I turned fourteen. Imagine a newborn not having milk, except for the breast milk, which too dried due to a mother's bad diet, and once that was dried out: nothing. I lived through it and I still can't believe it. You may be thinking, "Why didn't we use baby formula?" I don't think anyone knew there was such a thing anywhere. Not around us anyway. There was nothing at all.

Meat. Ah meat, such a foreign word. Meat was like a unicorn; we all believed it existed, but no one had ever seen it. The older generation remembered the times of abundance when they butchered their own animals they raised and took care of the meat, which was tasty. For people who were born after the collectivization—that would include me—meat was an imaginary concept. We only knew something that resembled it. Had I been asked to draw meat at that time, I would have drawn a bone that resembles the toys sold for dogs at the pet shop. Meat was sold at the same store where bread and milk were sold, except that there wasn't any. Every once in a while, they brought some meat at the store, rationed of course, and mostly bones, which wasn't enough to make one time stew, but it smelled like meat and looked like meat, so we called it meat. Meat came mostly from some animal that died and was butchered after. Most likely the animal died from a disease. As if eating dead animals wasn't enough, eating those who die from diseases are even worse, as they can transmit the disease to humans. God knows how strong our immune system must have been to endure all that unsafe food. Sanitary measures didn't exist and no one cared as long as we got fed. The animal was most of the time butchered in the open, then transported in an open cart pulled by horses or cows and dumped onto an open counter full of dust and filth. The store clerk did his best to ration it and give everyone a piece. If meat was brought in, the news traveled so fast, people ran like they were running for their lives. I thought a UFO was spotted when people were rushing in the street to go to the store. I always loved Abraham Maslow's "Hierarchy of Needs" theory. He professes that the basic human needs are food and shelter, and that until you have those, you can't move to the next stage. For forty-eight years, Albania never achieved the basic stage of Maslow's observation.

One thing was guaranteed, though: no one was ever obese.

In villages, most people owned their homes. My family had a house they had owned for generations. It was a two-story house built by my great great-grandfather. It had very low ceilings with narrow doors and windows, and there was a small balcony in front joined by an outdoor stairway. It was a nice house at the time it was built. However, the house had changed so much over the years that I could never figure out what was new to the house and what was original the original structure. When the house was built, the first floor was used as a cantina: and area for storing of dry foods and other stuff. Since we didn't have anything to store anymore and there was no use for it, it was converted into bedrooms to accommodate the large family. The ceilings were low everywhere, but on the first floor especially; an average person had to bend not to bump on the ceiling. On one side there was a living room with a fireplace. There were two small sitting wood benches with old cushions on top. A firewood stove stood in the middle in between the wooden benches that filled the role of sofa, and a dinner table was at the other corner of the room and pushed far away so as not to take up too much space. When dinner was served, we pulled it toward the center to accommodate us all. A small credenza occupied a small corner, where we kept the kitchenware. A kitchen, in its proper sense, did not exist. We cooked in the fireplace or the woodstove and washed dishes outside or at this very special place called "Sjoll." The stove was used only in the winter. For the rest of the year when it was warm, all cooking took place in the fireplace or outside in an open fire, like campers. One of the windows served also as sink. It was repurposed to have a basin area to hold water and had a drainage whole to let water outside. That is what we called Sjoll. Water went out of the window and flowed into the outside walls and disappeared into the ground or continued to travel down until it found a canal somewhere. All in the open.

To be clear, there was no running water anywhere in the house. No one in the whole town had any kind of plumbing in the house. Most of the country, in fact, lacked any plumbing and running water. On the second floor, there were three bedrooms joined by a very small hallway about 1x2 meters. Most of us slept on the floor for a long time, on some old mattresses filled with hay or old clothes chopped into small pieces to resemble cotton. The house was cold in the winter and hot in the summer. There were lots of mosquitos and no way of keeping them out of the house, so they bit us all night. During the "glorious" years of the Kooperativë, a large portion of the land was used to cultivate rice and that became heaven for mosquitos. From time to time a World War II single-engine airplane flew low as if it was going to hit the trees and spread some kind of chemicals, pesticides or alike. We were told that it was to kill the mosquitoes, but all it killed was our very few fruit plants we had around the house. So much for eating any grapes or figs that year.

Everyone in my family, apart from me and my older brother—both of us were still in school until the end of the regime—worked in a Kooperativë. My mother didn't work much at the time. She had worked a little in the early years, but then because she had many kids, she had managed to stay home constantly and was harassed and condemned by the local officials for doing so frequently. Having lots of kids was normal, but eight was a little higher than usual. Because of that, she had a compelling reason not to work. When harassments became unbearable, she went to work for several months and still fell back to staying home. There were also some good people in charge who closed and eye and let things slide. My father had made a choice to work harder and let my mother stay home. So mother was what we would call today a housewife even though she did much more than a housewife does today. She cleaned, cooked, washed clothes, and took care of the little vegetable garden.

The first order of business for her in the morning was to start the fire and make breakfast for everyone. Cooking was done in the woodstove or fireplace, and in the summer most of the time outdoors. She had to first procure the firewood, which was mainly fallen branches of trees; this resulted in more smoke than fire. She struggled with that fire all day, every day, all year, whether it was in the fireplace, woodstove, or outside. Her eyes were red and her face was black from the thick smoke that came from all directions. She had to constantly keep blowing at the fire to keep it going and managed somehow to keep it going all day to make breakfast, lunch, and dinner with just that single fire.

In the morning, it was chaos in our house. All the adults prepared for work and all the kids prepared for school. Adults were considered anyone above the age of fourteen, which included my brother and my three sisters before him. As soon as they had finished middle school, they were sent to work in the Kooperativë. They worked all kinds of jobs there, from digging ditches and canals to cultivating rice soaked in water, and this work was done all winter long without wearing boots to keep their feet dry.

Growing rice is a very tough job. The whole surface is constantly covered in water and most of the work was done manually: from spreading the seeds to collecting leftover grains at the end of the season. It was so unfeasible to spend so much time looking for some lost rice grains, but the Party decided it was worth it, just like it didn't make sense to ruin a perfectly fertile land and submerge it under water to cultivate rice when there was a natural swamp in Torovicë close by that was far more suitable for rice. Why spend money to drain the swamp and more money to flood the good lands? After cultivating rice, the lands get impoverished and it takes many years to be able to cultivate anything else. But did anything ever make sense in Communism?

My three sisters and my two brothers all worked pretty much the same jobs. Work in the Kooperativë was very close to slave work. People worked all day, rain or shine. Only when it came to some extreme weather conditions were they allowed to stay home. People were paid about one third of the normal pay for a rainy day, but who could complain? Anything you can get from the Party boss was a bonus. Everyone celebrated heavy rainy days when they were allowed to stay home. Rain was a double-edged sword. If it rained a lot, maybe they could stay home, but that decision depended on the whim of government leaders. For a normal work day, everyone had to carry lunch with them, being that they worked so far from home and were not allowed long breaks, that is, long enough to make it home for lunch. Usually, my mother would prepare the next day's lunch the night before for my father and siblings. Most of the time this lunch meant a piece of bread and some byproduct of milk extracted from cheese-making process, we called it "Kjumësht," and a bottle of water from the well. When making cheese, Albanian style, milk is boiled and some cheese-making magic chemical is used to create the cheese. After it cools off, the cheese separates and what is left is a liquid called "Hjerre." This liquid is tasteless, but after a while (a day or so) kept at room temperature it eventually becomes a little sour. This is what "Kjumësht" is: the lunch of my siblings working in the fields for ten hours a day. In rare cases, a piece of meat or cheese were available, or a cup of vegetable soup. Water got warm, but that was better than not having it. Many times the one bottle of water one can carry didn't last enough for the entire day, so they drank water from the irrigation canals or rainwater. Seems like describing a story of someone lost in the desert somewhere, but no: these were what the Party called the happy people of communist Albania in their best of times.

I can never forget the time when people returned home from working in the fields. The first thing they did was to run for water. We had a water well in our front yard. Everyone—well almost everyone—had one. That was the only source of water. The well was a hole about thirty feet deep and you had to toss a bucket with a rope to get water out from it. Since that well was the only source of water for everything, you can imagine how many times that bucket had to be tossed and pulled. Refrigerators were inexistent, so cold water was available only in the winter. That is fifty per cent success rate without any refrigerator, so not that bad. Actually, I don't think I even knew that such a thing existed until very late in my life. I think we bought a refrigerator sometime when I was fifteen years old.

During summer, you had to be inventive. That meant putting water in a shadow, keeping it under ground, or other sophisticated methods of the time.

Persecution worked at many levels. I can't even recall them all. It was a spiderweb that no one could keep tab. Starting with the fact that everyone in Albania was stripped of any basic human rights and all properties, there were other levels of misery not everyone had to endure. If you were born in a village, you were not allowed to move to a city, or another village for that matter. We were worse than trees. Even a tree can be moved to another place, provided it was situated in a similar climate.

People in villages were persecuted more than the people who lived in cities. If you lived in the capital city, Tirana, there were stores that in fact carried a little more products, but getting them was hard if you didn't live there. You had to show proof of residence and that was a dealbreaker. The residents had a special document called "tallon," another word and method barrowed from Russians. "Tallon" in Russian means coupon, but in Albania it was used a little differently. Why use an Albanian word, which sounds so bad on people's ears? Tallon sounded nice, caring, sophisticated, almost poetic. Tallon had become the most important document anyone possessed in the cities across Albania. Tallon was a piece of paper that listed everything a household can buy for the month and how much of each. Once you had used the allowance, you had to wait for the next month of borrow from friends and family and pay back next time. At some point it had gotten so bad, that my father and some other people from our town would take on journeys to travel to the capital to buy cheese. At the time, any cheese would have been great, but feta cheese is another product synonymous with Albanian cuisine. But like most other products, it was unavailable.

Going to Tirana at the time was not an easy undertaking due primarily to the lack of transportation. If you could make it to the capital and bribe the store clerks, sometimes they would sell you a can of feta cheese, about four kg, for a very high price—way above its value—in the black market style. That cheese would last for a very long time because when my mother cut a piece for us, it was so small I thought she would cut her fingers trying to make it as slim as possible. We didn't eat cheese; we licked it like an ice cream until it was no more. To this day, I still treat cheese with the utmost respect.

Traveling to Tirana was not an easy task, far from it. We lived one hundred kilometers from Tirana. That may not seem far today, but in a time and place with no transportation that was almost as hard as traveling across the continent. Also, in order to go to Tirana, we needed to go to Shkodër first, which meant the distance was augmented because Shkodër is north and Tirana is south of our town. First of all, you had to ask for two days off from work, which was not always easy to obtain, and you had to provide hundreds of excuses. We lived in a town that was twenty-five kilometers from Shkodër, the nearest major city with a train station.

This is how one could go to Tirana. You had to wake up very early, around three or four in the morning. Walk about five kilometers from home to the bus station to catch the six o'clock morning bus to Shkodër. Wait until two o'clock in the afternoon the train to Tirana. Get on the train to Tirana at two and arrive in Tirana at eight o'clock in the evening. The train would take six hours to cover one hundred kilometers. Buses and trains were so crowded because they were the only means of transportation, and so in most cases it was hard to find a seat. Lots of people were standing and packed like sardines. If you did get a seat, you would be sure to have several other people covering you from all directions with some sitting on your lap making it hard to even breathe. Because the stores were closed at this time, you had to find a place to sleep and wait for the next morning. Hotels were either not available or too expensive or both, so in most cases people slept in the park. Early the next morning go from store to store and find someone bribable and get the cheese. If you got the cheese, you had to hide it, because if spotted by police, you and the clerk who sold it to you both got in trouble.

Trouble could mean jail. Then you had to go back to the train station and get the next train to Shkodër. If you were lucky, you made it back at the end of day two following the same route. Basically, at the very best case it took two days to get a four kg of feta cheese. In many cases you came home without any because something didn't work out: there was no clerk willing to take the risk, the police spotted you and the cheese was confiscated, or someone robbed you on the way home. There were too many variables and all had to work perfectly or the plan would fail. But people didn't lose faith and persisted until the plan was a success. There were so many things that could go wrong, but if you made it, the entire family feasted for weeks at this achievement. Feast was simply symbolic, as the cheese had to be preserved and rationed carefully. It was a celebration of the achievement, not that any of the cheese was used for the occasion.

Apples and Oranges are Dead. Long Live Apples and Oranges.

Christmas was a thing of the past, as far as many were concerned, and as for me, that was a tale of a distant past, almost like Babylonian or Egyptian history. Christmas had been replaced by New Year's celebrations. Even the Christmas tree had been renamed the New Year's tree. New Year's, though, had become the most important holiday in the entire country. On the positive side, this was a non-religious holiday and since the country is a melting pot of religions, it united everyone once a year. I hate to give credit to the regime for anything, but I believe this here was one good thing. God knows if they had known we would like it, they would have banned it. They were not concerned with unity and happiness of the people but with the deepening of their misery.

When the New Year approached, we all looked forward to it. We decorated the house with some homemade decorations that consisted of colored paper cut in strips and stuck together to create a harmonious decoration. It was something. Another very important reason we looked forward to New Year's is that this one time a year, we had apples and oranges. While we had some figs and grapes in our small frond yard, there weren't any fruits available almost ever. New Year's is when the Party had deemed it appropriate to have people eat apples and oranges. I have no idea how this became a tradition, but apples and oranges were connected with New Year's like eggs are to Easter. On December 31st, to be exact, stores were supplied with apples and oranges. Everyone lined up early to get their share. In some years, the tradition would be broken and stores remained empty and so did the hearts of many break by the bad news after having spent many hours waiting for those cursed apples and oranges. How could they go home and tell their kids there were no apples or oranges this year? Many times my father would not wait to get the bad news around midnight but would think ahead and go to Shkodër, as did many others, and go on a quest to find the apples and oranges. I don't think apples have been so important to people since the Garden of Eden. Every store had supplies only for the residents of the neighborhood and it's not like you can go buy anything you want. Everything was rationed. But the store clerks found ways to sell some of it on the black market. Just like Jesus multiplied the bread and fish at the wedding of Cana, Albanian store clerks would double the amount of apples and oranges magically by stealing a little from everyone and making a true one kilogram more like a half a kilogram. This way everyone wins. Everyone gets apples and the store clerks get a little extra money. Many times, when I was still very young and I could not stay up until my father came home with apples and oranges, I went to bed disappointed.

When I tell people that I grew up in a small remote town, they think I had plenty of animals around. In fact, we didn't have any of them. Yes, there were animals, but they were property of the government. You were not even permitted to pet them. First, the government took everyone's land and livestock and made it common property, or better call it as is: the property of the government. After that, keeping any animals was illegal. If you wanted to have a pig, sheep, goat, or cow, that was illegal. It was as bad as having a tank or submarine at your house, or an atomic bomb. Periodically and in high secrecy, government officials conducted random searches to catch someone by surprise raising an animal for food consumption. A group of autocrats went from house to house and flipped everything upside down looking for any sign of *illegal* animals. When one hears the word "illegal" may be tempted to think of some exotic, endangered species protected by law, but we're not talking about that. We're talking about old-fashioned stinky pigs. If anything was found, it was confiscated and you were fined for illegal possession. Who would have ever thought that a pig could be so dangerous to socialism? Many of us did defy the government and did in fact raise a pig or two; otherwise, we would have died of starvation. You had to hide them and make sure no one, I mean no one, saw them, otherwise if the *counter-terrorism-elite-animal-finders* found out, that was the end of your pork for that year.

Mali i Jushit lies at the foothills of mount Barbullush, which is a low steep mountain. A natural hideout was one of the few blessings from God that worked in our favor, but we couldn't depend on it that much. Some dug holes inside our homes, some built bunkers, some built underground tunnels, and some used a spare room in the house to harbor these *terrorists*. They smelled so bad, but when we weighted the benefit of having a little pork while enduring the smell versus not smelling and starving, we chose the pork. Survival is the natural instinct that supersedes other senses. The will to live is a lot stronger than any hate for the pig's smell. We had learned to live with the smell that eventually we didn't even notice it. We masked those hideouts so that the officials could not find them. We cherished our pigs. We fed them well; as well as we could. Most of the food came from what we stole from the Kooperativë. To set the record straight: stealing from the government was not considered immoral or unethical. It was the complete opposite. It was considered a noble thing to do, even if what you stole you didn't need, because this was a way to reclaim some of our property the government appropriated without just cause. It was a way to weaken the regime as well, or so we thought. We did all we could to destroy the regime even if our actions did little to weaken it. I am proud to say that I took anything I could from the government property: lucerne, corn, cabbage, and whatever I could get my hands on. I wish Darwin had lived to see Albania during this period. He would have been so proud of his "survival of the fittest" theory in action.

This has been just a small window into my childhood, which can be used to describe the lives of most children in communist Albania.

When we talk about Communism today, at least at the time I am writing this book in the 2021, we think about Russia, China, North Korea, Cuba, Venezuela, and to some extent some Eastern

European countries: Poland, Hungary, or Czechoslovakia. We don't really think that one of the smallest Eastern European countries, Albania, would have been the symbol of the worst communist dictatorship ever existed, not in scale but by proportionality to the population. Stalin would be stunned to see how far the Albanian communists took his teachings and jealous he did not think of it before.

Living under Communism was like being at the hospital. Not only do you hate that you are sick and in pain, but there are constantly familiar noises that remind you of your location every time you try to close your eyes to take a short nap. The propaganda machine was set in motion and never stopped until the heart of the communist doctrine finally stopped beating and the head of the snake was cut off in 1992. For forty-eight years, the same tune played over and over again: Enver Hoxha, Party-Enver, Communism, Communist Party, Lenin, Stalin, Marx, Engels, War of Classes, Proletarian, Death to America, Death to Capitalism, etc.: these were the most commonly pronounced words everyone had to hear over and over again day and night at home, school, work, street, city, town, and every billboard on the side of the road. All music, arts, and literature were about the Party and its leaders. The Socialist Realism, as it was called, was the new and only genre in fine arts. Busts of Lenin, Stalin, Marx, Engels, Hoxha, even Mao Tse-tung of China, occupied the squares of cities and towns. The only newspapers available were those that the government owned and distributed. Same with television and radio. While the most notorious dictators of the world were glorified, America and England, among other countries without strongmen leaders, were vilified. When you think about it this is quite odd because America and England not only liberated Europe but helped Hoxha take power in Albania. *No good deed goes unpunished.* The mere mention of the word *America* in a casual conversation could land you in jail for a good twenty-five years.

There was something special about that "25" number. It was the "7" in a casino or like the Ace of Spades in a poker game. Not sure what made it so special, but communists loved it so much that used it more often than anything in sentencing anyone who didn't fall in line with the Party. They called this maverick behavior by many names, which were so familiar to everyone, because daily someone had to swallow the pill of a twenty-five-year prison sentence. Everyone in the country who could read had become a constitutional expert. The penal code was learned by heart by most. The range of punishment was wide open, from ten years to life. It was really easy: for everything you do, twenty-five years. When the crime was not in the penal code, it was labeled "axhitacion dhe propagandë"—agitation and propaganda or inciting insurrection. We hated these two

161

countries, England and United States, so much that we didn't even play in international sports competitions against them but had to let them win by default as a result of us not participating. Not that we were good at any sport but an easy win wasn't a bad deal for our adversaries. They didn't have to put on their jerseys or even sweat. With the United States I don't think we ever crossed paths in sports that I can think of, but with England we did, several times, being in the same continent. When the teams were drawn for the next tournament, we hopped we would not be on the same group with England because we knew that we could not play that game and that meant a lost opportunity. When the names of Albania and England were drawn from the same group, Albanian fans were very disappointed. Even though it was not very frequent, it did happen. It is fate. Fate had it for balls with the names of Albania and England to be in the same bowl where all the names of the countries are placed at random in one of six bawls where they were to be picked from. Fate had it that the young kid picked both of the balls with the names of Albania and England from that bowl. Fate had it for us to lose again. Everyone was devastated, not for the loss of the game as much because we knew we had no chance anyway, but for the missed opportunity to watch a soccer game. Sports were one of the very few pleasures left in communist life and that too was stripped away from us many times.

Being a target of the government was not without benefits. At least they provided us security against thieves or anyone who would want to harm us. Not that they were doing it intentionally to help, but it came as an added bonus given that many times our house was surrounded by Sigurimi (the secret police) and soldiers armed with Kalashnikov (AK-47) automatic weapons. They would come at random, or because someone had reported activity that seemed suspicious. Those claims were usually of the nature of "We spotted someone who looked like Kolë Marashi," the uncle who had escaped forty years earlier and now was an old man living in Yugoslavia. I doubt anyone of these well-wishers knew what my uncle looked like, but seeing a man around the house they didn't recognize was enough to associate him with a fugitive. Sometimes he would be a guest at a house they didn't know, and most times they simply made the story up for some favors or purely out of spite or to score some points with the regime. God knows what went on, as we were not supposed to know, but I remember being in the bushes around the house playing with other kids pretending to be a partisan fighter, when we would see real soldiers hiding in the bushes. If someone went out at night for whatever reason, mainly to go to the outhouse, we risked being shot without a warning. There was this one occasion where my first cousin, Mark, came very close to being shot if not for one of the local officials who recognized

Mark and stopped the soldier who was from the other side of the country from shooting an innocent man. Not only his courage to stop a soldier from shooting, but his swift actions, saved my cousin's life.

II.   Institutionalization

When you live in Albania and the highest honor you receive is a pin of Mao Tse-tung, you know something is amiss. Why not have an Albanian hero instead? The propaganda about Albanian identity and pride never stopped. All it did was work against it. The main squares were shadowed with Russian and Chinese Communist leaders whose names no one could pronounce as well as statues of Marx, Engels, and Hoxha. The idea of equality was played in such a way that it didn't make people equal, but institutionalized them. You can say equal in some way. The process started very early on and continued to the end. At some point, people who were born and raised in this regime and knew nothing better, became puppets, chess pieces, robots, or anything other than an individual. They were institutionalized.

Let's start with the names. You were not allowed to name your kids as you wished. This rule fell especially hard on religious-based names, such as the names of Catholic saints: Anthony, Peter, etc. They were all banned. There was a list of names provided and you had to pick one. It is customary to name the first-born son after the grandfather, for instance, and that didn't work. During the first years where new local registers of population were established, many families were forced to change their last names as well. In many cases, two brothers had different last names because they lived in different parts of the town, or different towns, or simply when they had to pick the last names, they hadn't been able to think alike. This was done in an effort to break large families and ties among relatives. A campaign of removing any traditions worked day and night. They were called "zakone prapanike"—outdated traditions and were heavily targeted. National costumes, musical instruments even, and other cultural identity objects were made widely unavailable, discouraged, and even vilified in most cases. It became unpopular to use them. It was shameful even at times. School kids were forced to wear the black apron with the red scarfs from the early ages. All aspects of life were changed in a way to create a unique oblique color that made everyone "equal": equally miserable. Everyone had to pledge allegiance to the Communist Party only. All greatness came from there. All history and literature books of prominent Albanians of the past were burned. Out with the old and in with the new. Except that the new was not so new, like a Bolshevik playbook that had been translated into Albanian. This can only be explained as the effort to institutionalize the society and strip them of any religion, national, family, and other values.

III.   Dress Code

There was a dress code everyone had to follow. Just like anything else, clothes were in a very short supply and even if you found something in the store, it was very expensive. Suffice to say, no one cared about the size as long as it fit somewhat close to one's body. No one even knew that clothes had size. Clothes were plain, dark and grey, with no colors. Very depressing, if you ask me, but so was life itself. Most people had similar or the same kind of clothes; it seemed as if everyone wore a uniform.

There were very strict rules of how clothes must be tailored. They couldn't be too tight or too wide or too short or too long or too low or too high. Since most of the time people purchased fabric and had the local tailor make clothes, being that it was the cheapest way and the most commonly available, these guidelines were very important and needed to be religiously followed. Gladly, the tailor was the best steward of these rules as they knew them best and could help you out in case you forgot any of them. If you asked for something to look fashionable, the tailor would ignore it and follow the guidelines instead. Anyone who didn't follow the guidelines was publicly criticized and punished. Punishments ranged from community service to internment camp or jail. At some point, a secret police special operations kind of task force were dispatched all over some cities and towns. Their task was simple: enforce the dress code established by the Party. Who knew the Albanian Government specialized in fashion as well? Government officials dedicated to preserving "correct" sartorial matters roamed around in plain clothes, and if they spotted anyone whose appearance was deemed improper, they would intervene and rip off their clothes and tape them with adhesive tape. The person was beaten and jailed. People were terrorized and were even afraid to walk in the streets for fear of becoming the next victim. On a daily basis we heard of cases where people were tortured in the middle of the city in plain daylight for wearing something that was not approved by the Party; these were people we knew, family members or friends or someone close.

Stores (or the only store in the entire town) were always empty. Only occasionally some new clothes came in. First the store clerk, a highly paid bureaucrat who had to be from the Party members with good standing, which meant they had to have proven themselves worthy of the Party's favors, took the new arrivals and hid them in the back and sold them at a higher price to anyone willing to pay. You had to bribe them, basically. Whatever was left, which was very little, was sold in a first-come-first-serve basis. People almost killed each other trying to get hold of the merchandise. The feud always resulted in a few happy customers but mostly sad ones. The sad ones included the ones who had saved enough money to buy a new piece of clothing for a son or daughter for a special occasion such as birthday, but were unable to be close enough on the line, and as soon as it was their turn, there was nothing left. It was even sadder for the ones who never had the money to even get that close and compete for anything. Just like when meat came to the store, the arrival of merchandise at the store made news fast. Before you can get to the store, it was mostly gone. I had to make sure to alert my parents in hopes they would get me some. I was disappointed more times that I care to remember. Either they had no money or didn't make it on time or some other reason. After some time, I stopped hoping they would get me something and simply treat it like a lottery ticket, where the odds are always against you. I can count on one hand the times I got something worth remembering.

Disappointment had become part of life. I stopped blaming my parents for being slow walkers and not being on time. I stopped blaming the store clerk for hiding most of the merchandise. I started blaming myself for being the youngest and the last one on line to get new clothes. Most people wore old clothes that had more patches than original fabric left. I was one of them. I reached the point where you couldn't figure out the original color or shape of the original cloth. Women of the house—wives, mothers, and sisters—got in trouble often when trying to find anything to patch the ripped clothes of their husbands, kids, and siblings. Even finding an old piece of fabric to patch something was hard. Good thing there was very little waste. No one ever let go of anything until there was nothing left of them. Even then, old clothes were repurposed for stuffing pillows or mattresses—for those who had mattresses or pillows, that is. Here we go again: Albanians—the pioneers of recycling and saving the environment

I might have had new clothes once or twice myself after everyone in the family lobbied my father for months to convince him to buy me new clothes at the beginning of the school year, and he was fast enough to rush to the store and discover that the clerk had not hidden them. Or maybe my dad had bribed him for it. Whatever the case, I couldn't wait for the school year to start so I could wear the new clothes. Those plain, black and grey clothes with no style had one appealing thing: they were new and because that is something we didn't get very often, we cherished them. The feeling of new was comforting and made me feel good and worth living for a change. I couldn't wait to show off to my friends and walked in with the head high and full of pride.

I remember once having new sandals and walking to school with my friend Sokol who stepped on my foot and tore off one of the straps of my new sandals. I cannot begin to tell you how sad I got and how long it took me to get over it. Maybe I never did, because I still remember as if it were yesterday—and it happened over thirty years ago! We were walking to school in this country road as we always did. At some point, there was a shortcut that went through a narrow passage. We did that to avoid following the longer path where the dirt road was. We had to walk in a straight line one behind the other on top of the side of an irrigational canal. Sokol was behind me and he stepped on my sandal. The leather strap ripped of the bottom and my new scandal broke. With it, my spirit broke too, and so did my joy of having those new sandals, something I had been looking forward for a very long time. How can any of it be replaced? It is as if something "money cannot buy" broke and it cannot be replaced. I never forgave my cousin for that. I always remind him every time we talk. Even now, after all this time, he never laughs at the matter, because he knows how devastated I was at the time and how much those sandals meant to me. He is a witness to my sadness that was partially caused by him, but most importantly, he is a witness of the hardship we shared. We were cousins and friends, and we were experiencing the same miserable life. We felt each other's pains and sorrows and we shared each other's joys, if there were any. I cannot recall anything in particular that sticks out as a happy time for either one of us, but had there been any, I am sure we would have shared it. Ah, yes, my new sandals would have been one of those happy times, but the happiness didn't last long. I think I will finally forgive Sokol for what he did. I know it was an accident and he felt terrible, probably as much as I did or more. He was a good boy and never caused any trouble. Fate had it that way and I will no longer hold it against him.

Clothes were not the only things to have strict guidelines. Do's and don'ts were part of every aspect of our lives. Everything had to be approved and when in doubt, you simply didn't dare do anything you were not extra sure was okay. Hair, for instance, was another aspect. Gladly for us, the barber was trained for the most part on what was acceptable and what wasn't, but then most of us never visited the barber. We couldn't afford it. The rest of us had to rely on a friend or brother or father to give us a haircut. Hair couldn't be long, short, or cover the ears. Sides had to be at a very specific location. There was in fact such a finite line that we called it the "Party's bone," which is the location of the cheekbone. Hair couldn't be lower than that. This was a style popular in the West in the 70s and our dear government had made sure to protect us from the infestation of any Western culture. Facial hair, such as beards were not allowed, but mustache was allowed for the most part unless local officials didn't approve of it. As you can see, the regime served as fashion experts on top of their other duties. Poor people: they worked so hard while wearing many hats. Of course, disobeying meant trouble and I'm not talking about a slap in the wrist. I'm talking about beatings, public humiliation, torture, and death.

IV.   Escaping the Regime

Some birds are simply not meant to be caged. It doesn't matter how many fences, walls, and fortresses one builds, there are simply no means to keep them caged. Birds are meant to fly free. I never understood this when I was growing up. I do understand now why the government didn't want people to leave the country if one didn't want to stay. For once, if people were given the choice of leaving, I can't think of many who would have opted to stay in Albania between the years of 1945 and 1992. After 1992 many people left as well, but that was mainly due to economic hardships and curiosity to see the world not persecution: that was immigration. Whenever I heard stories of such and such escaping the country, as infrequent as they were, I would wonder why they had to escape and not simply leave. Again, the term used was escape, like someone escapes captivity or jail. Life in Albania for the free people was similar to jailed persons in many respects, thus the term escape was the one best describing the act of one leaving the country. Let us make some simple comparisons between a jail and communist Albania. Jail is a confined space used to keep people who are sentenced to serve time for a particular crime. Albania was a place where citizens were sentenced to live under Communism by the great powers after World War II for committing the crime of being in the Eastern Bloc and as such, Albania would become Russia's piece of the pie to do what it pleased with her. Russia determined the type of government this country would have, just like it did in the rest of Eastern Europe. Many believed and still do that one of the biggest mistakes the Allies made after World War II was to leave Russia in charge of Eastern Europe. History has already shown that to be a huge mistake, but we will eventually forget how it came about and focus on the events of Russian influence during communist regime. People in jail are stripped of any rights. Everything is rationed. Albanians were striped of any rights, including but not limited to electing their leaders, free speech, free assembly, freedom of religion, and most basic human rights. Food and other necessities were rationed. A person in jail is limited to a confined living space. Albanian citizens were confined to the space of Albanian territory fenced with barbed electrified wire. They were also confined within their town or city and moving to live in another town or city was impossible, or nearly impossible. However, people who were connected to party leaders were favored to move around as they pleased. Leaving the country was completely out of the question for any reason. Passports did not exist. Growing up, the term passport was used for the identification card whose official name was "Letërnjofim." I learned about a real passport at the age of fifteen.

People in jail are always under surveillance. Albania was constantly under the watch of "Sigurimi," the Albanian Secret Police. Inmates are told when to wake up, sleep, and eat. Ordinary Albanians had very similar regiment. You were told what to do and when, day and night. If you tried to deviate, severe punishments were bestowed upon you. I remember an old man once saying, when he heard that a young guy was sentenced to fifteen years for saying the bread was awful, "We are all in jail, but he will have a smaller living space than us." He was right. Now that we have a better understanding of life in communist Albania, it would be not be as hard to understand why everyone would have wanted to escape. It also clarifies the reasons why the word *escape* was used to describe the act of one leaving their home country in pursuit of something else, anything else—but this.

Escaping communist Albania was anything but easy. People who managed to do so, were put on a very short list. We admired them, envied them, feared for them and their families, but dared not talk about them. These were the unsung heroes, the great warriors of a lost tribe. You didn't know what to say and to whom, because anything you said might have put you in trouble with the regime. We chose to say nothing and pretend things never happened, even though the act of one escaping was hard to ignore. Just like any other escape, escaping communist

Albania took lots of planning, secrecy, and courage. You had to be prepared to never see or speak to anyone you have ever known again. It was like going into a witness protection program—but without any protection. Your family, whoever you left behind— wife, kids, parents, siblings, and sometimes even extended family—would be sent to internment camps as a minimum and labeled the "enemies of the people" for the rest of their lives and their children's lives for as long as Communism lasted.

While heroes were very few apart, the victims list grew exponentially to infinity. Their lives would become hell inside hell. Deciding to escape, thus, was the hardest part of the whole act, as one could not condemn their family to the cruelty that was in store for them. Most cases I have heard of, understandably so, were people who had a life-or-death situation, and escaping was the only way to save their lives. The fact that there were severe punishments to the entire family of an escapee is why more people didn't leave but accepted their harsh fates, not because their courage was in short supply nor because the barbed electric wire may have killed them trying. It was not the fear of being shot or butchered by trained hungry military dogs. No. None of that would have stopped these desperate souls. In fact, it took greater courage to stay then escape. It was something far more important, something people value more than their lives: the family.

Although people didn't escape in large numbers, only a small number did manage to make it past the Albanian unmarked territory. Albania bordered Yugoslavia in the north and northeast via land, lakes, and rivers; Greece in the south and southeast via land; and Italy in the west via the Adriatic Sea. Albania now borders with Montenegro, Kosovo, and Northern Macedonia, which are all sovereign countries that used to be part of the Yugoslavian federation. Some rare cases are recorded of people making it to Italy, but most cases of escaping occurred on land that bordered Yugoslavia or Greece. A buffer zone, or DMZ (Demilitarized Zone), existed between the actual national border and the mainland. This buffer was out of limits for anyone without a permit, with the exception of people who lived in that area. The ones who lived in the buffer zone were supplied with special identification papers for the authorities to prove their residency. The buffer zone was about ten kilometers wide. If you managed to enter the buffer, there was the barbed electrified wire, and even if you managed to go as far as passing the wire, you were still in Albanian territory for another kilometer or so and chances you would get caught were very high. The only places not fenced where the ones high on the mountains where it was physically impossible to fence because it was either hard to fence the area, or the area was deemed impossible for anyone to cross.

Because everything was in short supply, and the government controlled anything and everything, attempting an escape to Italy was nearly impossible. The shortest distance between the two countries is forty-five maritime miles. You can technically cross on a rowing boat. But where to get the boat is the question. Even if one was to be procured, multiple layers of military guards were deployed, so getting near the sea unnoticed was out of the question. A similar buffer zone existed there too, and the security layers that were used for landlocked borders were installed. Now, adding the sea to the mix was just not something anyone thought of doing. Citizens were not permitted to own boats or anything that could be used as a floating device, thus, the Adriatic and Ionian seas were the most secure fences they could ever build. Seems even God had been on the side of the regime to give them such a great natural fence. I remember growing up and thinking of Italy being so far away, when in fact it is closer to Albania than it is to its own island of Sardinia. If you wanted to visit someone who lived in proximity to the borders anywhere (inside the DMZ), you needed permission from the police department, a kind of a visa. Every application was scrutinized and most people were denied. If you attempted to go without permission and got caught, the punishment was severe, so the minute you stepped in the area designated as a border, you were stopped by the authorities and then jailed and tortured. The charges were attempted escape and were considered treason.

Despite all this, some people couldn't resist the temptation to escape. If spotted in the area designated as border territories, most likely you would get shot on the spot by the police, army, or armed civilians who had permission to shoot to kill anyone who looked suspiciously like they were trying to escape. Albanian military and police, who are supposed to protect you, would shoot you like a strayed dog. Even your fellow citizens would shoot you without remorse. There have been several cases of people being shot while trying to escape. Some were caught alive and sent to jail, but not before being tortured for days, and their families would get picked up and sent to internment camps. Your life forward would be hell as long as the regime was in power. The ones who were shot were buried in unmarked graves and no one was allowed to attend, nor did they know their graves. Many have been forever lost and their families' grieving never ended. It's difficult to imagine just how many mothers have died with the unfulfilled wish to just know where the graves of their sons and daughters are, to be able to at least bring a bouquet of flowers, say a prayer, or cry their hearts out at their kids' graves. Many of them died heartbroken. Sometimes I would hear of such cases of people far from us and sometimes of people we knew of, and at times even of people we knew very well. Such was the case of two young guys: our neighbors, Dodë and Gjon.

Gjon was twenty-five years old when he got shot trying to escape. Gjon was the second-oldest son of Mark and Diellë. They were a simple family working hard day and night under the harsh conditions of Kooperativë to raise their nine kids. Kooperativë had a good connotation to it, almost romantic. It sounded good on paper. Everyone works together and helps each other. Everyone has exactly the same amount of everything. No one goes hungry. Everyone has a job. And so many other good things Kooperativë offered to make any country jealous. Issue is, though, it was anything but that. It was a plantation-style enterprise owned and operated by the government bureaucrats who rode in left over World War II Jeeps while everyone walked to work in mud and dust, rain or snow or sunshine. These bureaucrats resembled the SS guards of Auschwitz, while the laborers resembled a slave colony. If you lived in a village, you were sentenced to this life from birth. Like most of their friends, Gjon and Dodë had very little to look forward to in their lives besides this plantation. Gjon was a guy with a big smile. He didn't talk much and even when he did, his voice was low as if not to disturb something. Like most of his friends, he liked playing soccer, the only entertainment available to them. He was friendly and helpful. He lived with his parents and the rest of his siblings, as it was very common for anyone who was not married. He worked at the Kooperativë doing some of the hardest jobs there were. Cultivating rice was one of the least desired one, as far as I remember my older siblings say, and Gjon was always chosen to be there. He was a strong guy with wide shoulders and looked like a soldier from an ancient army. His family held no positions in the government, nor where they persecuted by the government. They were the typical neutral family with no ties to either side. They worked hard and maintained a good reputation in town. They were well-respected people.

Dodë was twenty-two years old. He was quiet and kept mostly to himself. I don't remember him much playing with the other guys on the soccer field, though I am much younger than him. He had a huge advantage compared to the rest of people in this town. His family had been able to send him to driving school and he had obtained a driver's license to drive trucks. At the time, no one owned a car and no one was allowed to own one. The only cars were the ones owned and operated by the government. Obtaining a driver's license was like having a college degree. Driving a truck was a pretty good gig. It paid well, you got to travel the country, and it was better than any job at the Kooperativë. I don't think Dodë ever got a job as truck driver, though because for that you needed some heavy weight connections. Dodë was the third of six kids of Fran and Mri. Dodë and Gjon were distant cousins. Dodë's family was very similar to Gjon's family. Basically, these young guys and their families were somewhat of the typical family of a small Albanian town. I remember them both growing up, although they were older than me, more my older brother's age, but still I knew them well. Our homes were about 500 yards from one another. This is a small town where everyone knows everyone and people are close to each other, especially in tough times such as these. Our families had lived near each other for more than 200 years.

These guys were not the most outspoken or front liners, or anyone you might think of someone with intensions and guts of taking such a step, yet to the surprise of most of us, they did it. They took that decision. "The hell with all this. Live free or die." That is what they must have had said to each other and their actions followed.

One summer early afternoon I returned home and everyone from my family and close neighbors was gathered and speaking in low voices. I could hardly make out anything they were saying, but their faces said it all. Their faces were gray as the clothes they wore and their expression was as yellow as the fields of grain lying ahead. Their shoulders were lowered to their knees and their jaws were wide open, some from crying and some from shock. Women were shedding tears, but dared not cry out loud. Men were angry and agitated, but held it together. Someone threw a shout or two at the government from "bastards" to "criminals" or even "I hope God will punish them for this." If reported to authorities, expressions like these would grant you a sentence of twenty-five years in jail, but everyone had had it and most didn't care if they were heard or not. That sentence alone had two elements that could land you in jail: mentioning God and badmouthing the government. Although none of the people around, mainly my family and close cousins, were blood related to the two young guys in question, they were "our boys," as someone put it, from the same town, our next-door neighbors. These were people we shared everything with. They were like sons and brothers to us all. Most importantly, this was another reminder that it could happen to anyone. Anyone was our friend against the monsters of the communist regime where everyone had had just about enough. It is 1998 and the roots of this communist cancer had started rotting already. But like most monsters do, they unleash their last attacks upon their death. They become more ferocious and unpredictable. The communist beast was about to die soon, but not before it claimed its last prey.

Everyone was upset because of terrible news had been spread: Gjon and Dodë were shot at the border trying to cross the river of Buna into Yugoslavia. They were not shot by our historical enemy, Yugoslavia, but by our own army who is supposed to protect us. Our military had shot dead two of the finest young men I knew. Their only crime was that they couldn't take it any longer and wanted to leave the country to pursue something better, something more humane. These birds could no longer be caged, but their wings were cut off and their dreams of flying never realized. Their lives were cut short in their prime youth. How could anyone *not* be sad, angry, and outraged?

Everyone was talking, and while details were unknown to most, one thing was certain: they were dead. As the minutes passed, as slow as the currents of a frozen river, more details became available. As if killing these two poor souls was not enough, the regime had taken their dead bodies and stripped their clothes off, tied them behind a military vehicle covered in frozen blood and dust. An inscription, "Armiqtë e Popullit"—The Enemies of The People written in white chalk hanged above their bodies at the back of the vehicle. They were taken from one town to another in the whole region where people were gathered to see and "learn the lesson" of what happens to those who dare to try. They were paraded like Jesus on the mount of Calvary carrying the cross and being spat on. They were shown to everyone, including children. Some courageous local leader spared the family the horrific sight and did not allow the show to be carried on their hometown.

Many people fainted at the horrible sight and couldn't speak for days. I need to remind you this is 1988 Albania and not the Second World War of Nazi Germany or anything else from far past history. This is not a tale I heard. This is something I lived. This is the time where people had already been to the moon and back many times. This is in a country in the heart of Europe surrounded by nightlife and casinos, yet atrocities such as these were commonplace in Albania, unknown or uncared for anywhere else outside the country.

As more news became available, the more that anger grew, and the more people gathered around to discuss. First it was only the family, then it became the whole neighborhood, and then the whole town was quickly in shock. For the longest time, there was nothing else discussed around the dinner table. It wasn't even what was said over and over again. It was the unspoken words of anger and sorrow that I would never forget.

After the parade of their naked bodies was concluded and the terrifying of many people had stopped, their bodies were buried, or better, dumped like garbage in a common unmarked shallow grave somewhere in the wilderness where no one knew except for those who were responsible for the act. Their families were denied the right to give a proper burial or grieve for them. Even crying had to be done in secrecy. How can one mourn an "enemy of the people" who had committed the ultimate crime of treason?

Town meetings followed shortly after where government officials bashed at them and cautioned others to be careful and not follow their footsteps if they didn't want to experience a similar fate. Their families were forced to endure all this and make no objections nor express any discontent. They sat silently in those meetings and bit their lips, tongues, fingers or whatever could make them hold their tears from running. I can hardly find anyone at those meetings who approved, but for the close ones, being there was a torture. Of course, not going to the meeting was not an option either. In these parts of the world, mourning the dead is done according to certain rituals that are passed on from generations. One of them is to dress all in black for a period of time, usually one year or more depending of the age of the deceased, to let everyone know that you are mourning. Apparently, the families of Gjon and Dodë did just that, but this didn't go unnoticed and the government officials got to work. All family members were called to report to the local police station where they were criticized for mourning the "enemies of the people" and were ordered to remove any signs of mourning immediately. They were warned not to repeat it again, or else. Everyone complied and went home. The communist eye kept close watch on them for a long time to come. Thank God the end of Communism was close and the pain would ease for these families and the savagery of this sort would soon end for everyone else.

It was not until 1992 that the remains of our boys will be uncovered and a proper burial would take place. The day of their reburial was a sad one, even more so than the day of their death four years earlier. Now, people were free to speak and no one stopped short of calling the communists "murderers" and other names out loud. The funeral reminded everyone the hard life they had recently broken from, a life everyone wished would never happen again to anyone anywhere in the world. As I am writing this, unfortunately, many parts of the world are still under harsh communist regimes or other forms of oppressive dictatorships, with North Korea as perhaps the most oppressive of all. Human cruelty knows no boundaries. Lessons learned quickly fade away in the waves of time, and people fall prey to scrupulous dictators. I guess lessons are never learned. They are only studied and forgotten.

V.   Family Separated by Ten Kilometers

With the establishment of borders in a hurry between Albania and Yugoslavia, many families were separated, much like the Berlin Wall separated Berliners living on both sides of the wall. Had they known what would become of them, I am sure they all would have tried to be on the western side of this wall, but by the time it that was made known it was too late. It all happened so quickly that there was no time to think. You're in or you're out. That was the reality of family separations.

Another scenario, and there were many cases, concerned women who were married and their family happened to be on the other side. They were condemned to never see their families again.

And then there were the people who had escaped and lived close to the Albanian borders, such as my uncles, Kolë and Gjekë, who had chosen to settle in Ulqin, Montenegro (ex-Yugoslavia), a city on the coast of Adriatic Sea close to the border of Albania. Not only is this city close to Albania, it is an Albanian city with majority of Albanian habitants. Via air, the distance is about ten kilometers from our home. By car, it takes about one hour. It is that close yet it seemed so far away as if it were in a different planet. My uncles had escaped and now were living a free life in the neighboring country. This was a small victory, but the war was far from over. The only means of communication with them was letters. Kolë and Gjekë got married and started their families in Yugoslavia. Kolë had one girl and two boys. Gjekë had two boys. Even during the seventies when many people from that part of the world migrated to United States, my uncles decided to stay in hopes that one day the regime would collapse, which would allow them to go home. Their escape was not a wished one, but forced by the brutal dictatorship of Albania's merciless communist regime. They were allowed to send letters and we exchanged a lot of them over the many years. We shared major events, such as births, weddings, even deaths of loved ones. We were constantly under surveillance and all the mail was read, so we had to be very careful in getting political in any way. They knew it too and the silent protocol was to stick to family affairs. It worked for the most part. We had this kind of platonic love that lasted for the entirety of their lives. Gjekë passed in 1983 and Kolë in 1991. Kolë almost saw the day where he can come home, but didn't make it. He never saw his beloved country again. When my brother Marash escaped to Yugoslavia in 1990, he was the first person from this side of the family to see the other side. It had been so long that my first cousin, born in Montenegro, was now forty years old.

When a letter arrived from them, the whole neighborhood gathered to read it. We also exchanged pictures from time to time, but didn't dare put them on display when we received pictures from them. Telephone calls were not allowed, even though there was one telephone on the town that technically could be used at least once. As far as the regime was concerned, letters were the only means of distant communication. We made do with that stricture as best we could.

4. The Wall Has Fallen

"Mr. Gorbachev, tear down that wall." Those words pronounced by President Ronald Regan during his historical speech in West Berlin on June 12, 1987, shook the core of the cement of the Berlin Wall with a more powerful force than any machinery ever built by mankind. Those words trembled the foundation of that wall built with the finest cement and Russian steel with much greater power than the Atomic Bomb hit Hiroshima and Nagasaki. Those words echoed at the Kremlin, not only Gorbachev's ears but in those of communist dictators everywhere. For many, June 12, 1987, will be reminded as the beginning of the end of the communist era in Eastern Europe. It then took almost two more years before the Berlin Wall was officially dismantled, on November 9, 1989. A piece of the wall was donated to New York City and placed in my neighborhood in Battery Park as a reminder of Communism. Most people pas by and ignore it, but I could never pass by and not stop and reflect.

The communist governments begun to fall like dominoes one after the other in many countries of Eastern Europe: not without claiming more lives in the process. The two German countries were united, Czechoslovakia was separated into the Czech Republic and Slovakia, and the Soviet Union was

195

dismantled. Yet, the communist regime in the tiny country of Albania was still holding on to its power—just a little longer. In fact, the late 1990s marked some of the most brutal acts of atrocities committed by the communist regime of Albania. These years resulted in the largest number of murders at the borders of Yugoslavia and Greece where people tried to escape in droves. Politically and economically, the country was on the verge of collapse and the belts of citizens were getting tighter and tighter until it could go no more. Oblivious to all of this, the communist leaders of Albania were still proclaiming that the country was indeed in a healthy state and everything was on the right track to achieving the communist utopia, the final stages of greatness as professed by Marx and Engels.[23]

But people were not having it anymore. They had reached the end of their ropes and couldn't take it any longer. Emboldened by the events elsewhere in Eastern Europe, people finally started to rebel against the government and began demanding freedom and liberty. Several events marked the fall of Communism: taking down statues of Stalin in the city of Shkodër, street protest in the city of Kavajë, storming embassies, and the exodus to Italy. Ironically, the removal of the statue of a foreign leader, Stalin, was the first shot fired in the long struggle

---

[23] *The Communist Manifesto*, written by Karl Marx and Frederick Engels, the playbook that was being used to keep people in dictatorship, states that Communism is the highest state of socialism where everyone will eat with a golden spoon.

for freedom from Albanian communist oppression. Although isolated cases of some rebellion were recorded sporadically throughout the country, the first organized protest occurred in the city of Shkodër on January 14, 1990.

Shkodër is the third-largest city of Albania and the largest city of northern Albania. It has served for centuries as the center of trade and commerce for northern Albania and parts of Montenegro. In the city center stood a statue of Russian dictator Joseph Stalin, who murdered and imprisoned more Russians than Hitler did during World War II. Despite that, his statue was installed in the city center of Shkodër and had been there for several years: it had become a landmark. Even Russians had somehow fallen out of favor with him, but not the Albanian communists who revered Stalin so much that his name, portrait, or statue were found everywhere: in government offices, classrooms, engraved in the valleys, on the side of the main roads, and billboards across cities and towns. Hundreds of people gathered around the statue to ask the removal of his statue that had "stained the city" of Shkodër. From a silent protest, things escalated and crowds turned to the large statue with everything they had and took it down. Police and military didn't stand idle, as it was to be expected, and many were beaten and arrested. That didn't stop people from protesting and instead of putting the protests down, these acts of police violence further incited them. People took to street in even larger numbers for many months to come and years to come until it was all over.

Kavajë on March 26, 1990. Fueled by the events of other Eastern European countries and protests in Shkodër, Albanians finally took to the streets in other cities, in particular Kavajë in central Albania. It all started during a soccer game at the stadium where people began chanting anti-communist slurs and calling for freedom and democracy. Many people were arrested. Demonstrations continued on the streets demanding the release of the ones arrested in the stadium. The situation escalated and a major protest quickly spread in the whole city. The chronological events of this major uprising were hidden to public by the regime, but we knew at the time that there were several dead and wounded by the bullets of secret police, national guard, sniper fire, and God knows what else that was deployed in secrecy by the regime.

Without a well-documented chronology, it is hard to tell what happened when, but chaos took over quickly and order was lost. On June 23, 1990, a truck driven by a brave soul by the name of Fatos Kaceli drove into the main gate of the Italian embassy in Tirana tearing it down and opening the path for people gathered around the embassy to enter the premises. His act was followed shortly after by masses of people following in his footsteps, and one embassy after the other was stormed by thousands of citizens seeking political asylum. On July 2, 1990, several thousands of people had broken into foreign embassies fighting their way through in bloody confrontations with the military and police. They climbed tall fences, broke heavy metal gates, climbed with ropes, or ladders. The scenes resembled the siege of Troy more than a modern-day protest in a capitol city in the heart of Europe. The Albanian government demanded that the respective countries hosting these refugee seekers extradite them to Albania, which meant kicking them out of the premises right into the mouth of the hungry communist beast, but their requests were refused. Even though for many days and weeks several thousands of people wandered inside the fortified embassies with little food or water, they refused to give up. After many days of negotiations, asylum seekers were airlifted from embassies to the Rinas International Airport and the Port of Durrës, and from there their safe passage to the respective European countries was secured. This was a huge blow to the communist government. One protest after the other, one city after the other: eventually the entire country rebelled. Students took to the streets supported by some professors. A doctor and professor unknown to most until then by the name of Sali Berisha emerged in support of the student rallies, and the communist dictator, Ramiz Alia, agreed to sit and hear their demands. He ordered a list of reforms trying to calm the angry protesters, but that had very little effect. He appointed himself "President" of Albania and agreed to legalize the creation of other political parties and hold an election. The first opposing political party created was "The Democratic Party of Albania" and Sali Berisha was appointed the leader of it.

Albanians had a clear view of who they wanted out and who they wanted in. They wanted the communists out and Sali Berisha in. The Democratic Party promised to return freedom and human rights to Albania and bring the country closer to the West. He was our savior, our Noah, our Moses, our Messiah. He was our George Washington because up until now, for a long time, every government was installed by force. Some were occupying foreign governments and the last one, although Albanian, was a dictatorship. Sali Berisha and his party were created by the pressure student demonstrations put on the government. This party was not created from oppression or as a post-war de facto installment. While not perfect, this seemed a dream come true. Sali Berisha seemed genuine, and spoke eloquently and candidly. Even if the masses didn't really understand the pluralist system that they were all chanting for, they just knew that something better ought to be out there. Anything but Communism.

After few years of struggle, Communism fell, finally, and Sali Berisha became the first democratically elected President of Albania in March of 1992. I was still in my teenage years. After the regime was gone, our lives began to improve drastically. Every Kooperativë was dismantled. The land was equally distributed to the members of each town and all the livestock as well. Most of property owned by government was also distributed evenly among the people. My family received five goats, five sheep, and one cow. For the first time in my life, I could drink enough milk. Now, the government cannot tell me how much milk I can get: my cow, sheep, and goat will make that decision. That was a huge achievement. For many days I ate nothing but bread with milk for breakfast, lunch, and dinner. I felt like the person lost in a desert for many days seeing water for the first time. I just could not get enough of it. Oh, how good milk tasted! This was pure milk, straight from the source, not the milk government gave us. For the first time I learned what real milk looked and tasted like.

They say justice can be delayed but never denied. I don't think that holds any truth since generation after generation have died in hope of getting justice, but justice never came. If we can agree that justice after death is acceptable and fulfills the prophecy, I concede, but I believe justice is served only when the victim can see it. Posthumous justice is not justice: it only brings closure to the victim's family. They also say hope is the greatest motivation in the world. It's what keeps people alive even in the worst of circumstances and conditions. Hope keeps people alive even when everything else is lost. It is hope, then, that one can credit for how people have survived a regime of extermination, famine, and persecution of unprecedented nature in Albania. Even when hope seems to have abandoned us, we still called upon it in times of desperation when nothing else had worked.

At the beginning of 1990, after the fall of Berlin wall and the breakup of the USSR, Albanian communist roots started to tremble as well. Several events took place that marked the beginning of the end of communist regime. A much-awaited freedom finally was close and people dared to dream again. There was light of the end of the tunnel, although the tunnel was very long. I, too, made my contribution to my country's freedom by going to the main square of the town center and screaming my lungs out calling for the end of Communism. I learned later that what I was doing was considered a protest. What did I know what a protest was? No one dared protest before. The Communist Party was the mother party; how could we rebel against it? For the first time in our lives, we dared to loudly criticize the government. At first, we heard about the Berlin Wall. We rejoiced, but couldn't dare do it out loud. Then, protests erupted in major cities. Then it came to major towns. And then it was everywhere. Word spread quickly and I joined the group of youth from my town and headed to the center of municipality in Barbullush where the rally was taking place. Someone of importance from the new Democratic Party that was just created spoke to the crowd and the crowd exploded in calls for freedom, democracy, and death to Communism. He wasn't able to say more than a sentence without being interrupted by loud cheers that could be heard from our home four kilometers away. I waved a sign made from carton box paper that read "Liri – Demokraci," Freedom – Democracy. Many others held similar sings and flags. There were many Albanian flags that lacked the communist star[24] while some other people waved American flags. Many people were imprisoned, beaten, tortured, and killed. Tanks roared in the streets of cities and towns with their cannons lowered at street level where the only weapon of the opposition side was a handful of exhausted citizens throwing rocks and calling for the end of the communist regime. It was a scene repeated many times throughout history: a picture painted and photographed repeatedly, but now very close to home. I remember one instance where the tank driver who was patrolling the streets of Shkodër in an attempt to disperse the protesters saw

---

[24] During Communism, the national flag of Albania was altered by adding the white communist star to the black double-headed eagle on the red background.

his own brother on the other end of the metal window of the tank. Faced with what would have been probably the biggest decision of his life, given that he had orders to shoot, the military brother abandoned the tank and joined his brother in the street. We also gathered around the radio and listened to Voice of America and Vatican Radio broadcasting in Albanian to make sure we didn't miss anything.

Total collapse ensued. Not only was the political system rotting, the economic aspect was collapsing as well. The country was going bankrupt. After many years of isolation and economic regress, finally it came all to an end, an end that most had hoped for but doubted it would ever become reality. While the country was in a state of chaos, we would sit in front of the television impatiently waiting for the communist leader, Ramiz Alia, to talk to people. To our dismay, even though everyone knew the end was near, he would still continue to play the same tune played for forty-six years straight: the same lies, deceits, and propaganda. And then one evening, he made a stunning revelation. The forceful leader who had always proclaimed the goodness of his leadership and the communist doctrine told the people that the country had only three months of food supplies left. Because the government was the only source of everything, this meant starvation was near.

For the next two years, at least, we were fed, clothed, and medicated with supplies brought by many humanitarian organizations and foreign countries, most notably the Italian Military. The famous operation coded "Pelican" was set in motion, thanks to a very good neighbor, Italy. A pelican is a bird that will sometimes feed chicks that are not its own. Italians were feeding Albanians; thus, the name "pelican" was chosen for this mission. Pelican mission has remained in Albania as one of the most important historical events of the post-communist era. I remember vividly going on the main road with my friends to marvel at the military convoy passing through to bring food to us. It is a vivid remembrance of those days of struggle and support from a country we had bashed for forty-eight years. Thanks, Italy!

I.   My Brother's Escape

I am the youngest of eight and the second youngest child is my brother Marash, who is three years older than me. He and I were very close in age and also in physical appearance such that sometimes were mistaken for twins. Marash was smaller for his age and I was somewhat bigger for my age, closing the gap a little. Marash, like most of my siblings, was a top student in school. Yet his future seemed so bleak. It was a known fact that being from a family such as ours, you were not allowed to pursue higher education. The highest education possible was high school. There were two types of high schools: professional (prep) or agricultural high school. The one we could attend was the agricultural high school, the one that trained people for farming, besides the usual communist propaganda classes.

Going to college was a hard thing for just about anyone, as the government decided how many would go to college, who they were, and what they would study. In the majority of cases, there were two spots every year for the whole town of 13,000 people. The subject of study was chosen, and if you lived in a Kooperativë, it was almost always veterinarian or agricultural specialist of some sort. This was to ensure that after college you come back to your hometown, to be sentenced to live where you are born. That was the idea. Who were these two lucky ones who went to college? Kids of highly regarded members of the communist elite. Good grades didn't matter, a good family name did. And by a good family name I mean by communist standards. Marash loved to study more than anything else. The only other thing he liked maybe as much was playing soccer. He was damn good at it too. That too was forbidden for him and the likes of him. He would never play professionally for any team as long as this regime was in power, so he was content to play with friends only. Such a waste of talent, I think.

Marash hated the life he was subjected to and never hid his disdain. At the age of five he was charged with a misdemeanor offense for taking a sunflower from Kooperativë property. He was trialed and fined for it like some drug lord. The whole town was gathered to watch: some with curiosity, some despising the process, some in disbelief, and yes, some enjoying the whole spectacle. We had many enemies and they weren't afraid to show it. As a matter of fact, they wanted us to know it. It gave them much pleasure to see us suffer. Our enemies were die-hard communists or pro-communists rotten to the core with the will to destroy our family and they didn't spare even small children. One such child was my brother Marash, who would never forget that time, nor would I.

In January of 1991, Marash was in his third year of high school. He was by far the top student. He was so good that even the elite had to admit it. He shined when it came to math, science, history, and all other subjects. He even aced the much-hated subject taught in all schools, "Marxism and Leninism," which was the doctrine of Communism. He also did well with the Russian language, which we despised simply because anything Russian equated to Communism. He did it because he needed to prove that he was worth it. That didn't matter, anyways. "I am sorry, but this is the law" or "I wish it were up to me" were some common responses to his requests for higher education requests made to local bureaucrats and teachers alike. Communism had started to shake at its core by now. The Berlin Wall had fallen and many Eastern European countries had started to overthrow their communist regimes, but time was running out for Marash who only wanted to study. The future was very uncertain. Some events had already taken place in Albania and people had started to escape in much higher rates than before. Merely sixteen years old, he joined a group of much older and much more capable guys who had decided to take their chances and escape the country. Marash had a small body and looked no more than thirteen, but his intelligence surpassed any of the companions of this undertaking. He knew science and math and put them to good use during this escape that the team so much needed. Marash decided to leave and there was no backing down. One cold winter morning, on January 21, 1991, when I woke up, I realized that he wasn't in the room we shared. Where might he have gone? We looked everywhere and asked everyone, but no one seemed to have any information on his whereabouts. Later in the day we learned that other people from the same town were missing. These were all on the same group of soon to be added to the infamous list called "enemies of the people," the ones who dared to escape the Albanian inferno. My older brother Rrok confirmed that Marash had confided to him his plans but had sworn to secrecy. Rrok had tried to convince him to not do this, but eventually wished him luck after giving him some money for the journey.

The group of "enemies of the people" had made it to Montenegro by dawn going through the same process of cutting through the barbed wire and avoiding being seen by the patrol or sensed by dogs. They were exhausted but somehow relieved. Marash would spend his next nineteen months between refugee camps of Montenegro and Serbia that were administered by the United Nations and funded predominantly by United States.

The Serbian hate for Albanians runs deep and they are not shy about it. The refugee camps were run by the Serbian criminal government of Slobodan Milosevic who mistreated these poor souls for the only crime of being Albanian. It seems they couldn't find peace anywhere. First, they were put in a jail with common criminals for three months. Then later they were put into refugee camps for another six months with about sixty people in a small room whose size was approximately four-by-four meters. Food was bad and never enough, and the guards would beat them up regularly. NATO would later bomb Serbia in 1999 for the atrocities committed in Kosovo, an Albanian province under Serbian rule (Kosovo later became independent in 2008).

After one month in prison in Belgrade, the United Nations released Marash and allowed him to go live with his paternal uncle Kolë, the very one who had escaped in 1948. Now an old man, Kolë had almost lost all hope at ever seeing any family member again, and seeing Marash at almost the same age Marash's father and Kolë's brother were at the time of his escape, was a miracle. Marash lived in Ulqin for another nine months while waiting for a response from the United States government on his asylum application. He returned to Belgrade to be interviewed at the United States Embassy. His asylum request was denied and so he ended up staying in a refugee hotel in Belgrade along other Albanian refugees again.

He appealed the decision to his request to the United States Embassy in Austria, which had jurisdiction over Marash's case. His appeal did it and his asylum was approved. Finally, on August 27, 1992, he entered the United States with refugee status. All this happened during the war in Yugoslavia, which led to a dismantling of the country. As a result, there were no flights in and out of Yugoslavia, so a UN representative from a refugees office was sent to Belgrade and escorted Marash to Hungary. They traveled to Budapest, Hungary, by train and from Budapest Marash flew to the United States. Marash earned a PhD from Columbia University in NYC in 2010. His thirst for knowledge was finally satisfied and a sense of gratification sent chills throughout his body. He was vindicated.

The day it became known that Marash had escaped, I had the worst day in school. The principal, some teachers, and the local communist leaders came to my class and pulled me out. They took me to the principal's office and interrogated, threatened, and verbally abused me for hours. They were mad with questions: How can someone at his age manage to escape? How did he fool us all? It's ironic that this was the first time I ever stepped foot into the principal's office. Being the good student as I was, I had never had any business there. This was the first and the last time I ever went there and it wasn't because of something related to school or my behavior. No, my behavior was kosher and my academic records were impeccable. I had committed a far worse offense. I was the brother of an "enemy of the people" and that put my name much higher on the "most hated" list, as if being the son and nephew of other "enemies of the people" wasn't enough. This confirmed that a new generation of sworn enemies of Communism was being groomed from this family.

II.   The Grand Exodus

Exodus has always been the best word to describe the population's desire to flee its own country—and the events surrounding my brother's escape to Italy. It's a powerful Biblical term that captures the events of March 1991. Even though only 30,000 or so people made it safely to Italy, hundreds of thousands of people stormed the major ports of Albania hoping to get on to one of the ships sailing to Italy. The area in and around the ports looked like a beehive with people climbing, walking, crawling, jumping and making any possible attempt to get into one of the ships. It seemed that everyone in the country was gathered in one of the three ports: Shëngjin, Durrës, and Vlore.

That same year Marash escaped via land to Yugoslavia, another brother, Gjergj, took his chances at escaping via sea to Italy. He was serving mandatory military service in Lushnjë County. He had completed eighteen months out of the two-year time required. Gjergj was always a maverick. He always managed to upset the regime with acts of disobedience such as keeping his hair longer than allowed or listening to foreign music on his portable radio. He got punished several times, but always went back to his disobedient ways.

At the age of fourteen he started working in the Kooperativë and was assigned to the hardest tasks. This was no doubt due to my family's background and because Gjergj was a non-conformist. He hated the regime with all his heart and always talked about escaping. He never tried to escape, but I'm sure he would have done it one day after being discharged from military service, but fate brought him into the Port of Durrës at the right time and right place on March of 1991.

His journey began on March 6, 1991. He had been home on leave for a week. Early morning, we hugged goodbye with him and he took off on foot to the nearest road where he needed to find transportation to Lezhë, the nearest train station about thirty kilometers away. After an hour's walk, he made it to the main road. There he boarded a truck to Lezhë and then took a train from there bound to Lushnjë, where he was stationed. The train stopped in Durrës, which was also the train hub but wasn't allowed to proceed further. One of the biggest uprisings was taking place where people had stormed the ports and stopped all the ships that were docked there and ready to set sail toward Italy across the Adriatic Sea. He was in the middle of the exodus. Ships were so overloaded that there was hardly any space, so to make room they threw merchandise into the water—and some people as well. Some climbed onto the ship's masts. Some fell and were injured or even killed. On the ground, the military and police were firing shots, some in the air and some to kill. Some ships were loaded so much they couldn't even start. Train locomotives were used to pull them from the docks (the train tracks ran parallel to the docks). This uprising/escape took place for three days. Many ships made it, many drowned, many returned back because they were old or overloaded. With complete chaos happening on the ground, Gjergj decided to go back to Lezhë and stay overnight at my sister's home and try again the next day.

The next morning, he was back on the same train going to Lushnjë. The train arrived in Durrës station at 2:00 in the afternoon and wasn't allowed to proceed further. This time, Gjergj decided to join the party. Between 2:00 P.M. and 6:00 P.M. he struggled but made it on to one of the ships. The vessel was so overloaded it couldn't move from the dock, so several locomotives were used to help it set sail. Finally, at 4:00 A.M., on March 7, the ship left the port. Around midnight, between March 7 and March 8, the ship docked in the Port of Brindisi, Italy. He made it to Italy after a long thirty-hour journey at sea. He was hungry, thirsty, exhausted, and worried about what would happen next. If sent back, he would surely be court martialed or worse. *What would happen to us, his family? Would they be sent to internment camps? Will I see them again?* These and so many other questions got him pondering as he sailed toward the unknown. Nothing was certain, except for one thing: life had forever changed. Other parallel events had started to take place in Albania where mass anti-communist demonstrations paralyzed the country and the communist government was forced to accept political pluralism and hold elections. Some of the known practices, such as those of sending people of escapees to internment camps, were paused, so we were spared yet another wave of internments. We were somewhat safe, but uncertain. Every day we waited for someone to come and take us. That day never came. On top of it all, we had no information about Gjergj for months. He had landed into a refugee camp in South Italy with very little way to communicate with us. Not to mention that Albania was still a closed society and the likes of him were still considered enemies and not allowed to communicate back. Keep in mind that the country's infrastructure was still 1950 technology with one telephone available for the whole town. The telephone was broken most of the time.

Italians are a gregarious, warm-hearted people who have taken in thousands of people who landed on their shores. They clothed them and fed them for months. The government was overwhelmed and the emergency teams were unprepared for this event, but civilians took matters into their own hands and no one was left out to dry and go hungry. It's estimated that thirty-thousand people crossed the Adriatic Sea in three days. Albania should and will be eternally grateful to this nation.

Eventually, we got word that Gjergj was safe and sound in Italy. He wasn't sent back. He wasn't court martialed. We were never deported anywhere. Communism would soon collapse and we will all reunite soon in happier days. Gjergj still lives in Italy with his wife and three kids in Como Lake. He is a proud Italian citizen and his family enjoys life in this beautiful country.

The fall of Communism found my family in three countries: Marash in United States, Gjergj in Italy, and the rest of us in Albania. At some point, my entire family, including all my siblings and parents, left Albania and we all now live in Italy and United States. Though Communism has fallen, the bitter taste is still fresh in our minds.

III.   Becoming a Catholic at Last

I come from Christian family. My family is Roman Catholic on my mother's and on my father's sides. It has been this way for my family as long as Christianity has existed in Albania. Religion, not just for my family but for most Albanians, is more tradition than faith. Communism and religion didn't get along very well anywhere, but in Albania the communists took it a step further. They outlawed religion of any denominations and Albania was declared the only atheist country in the world in 1968. The country's leaders had decided to just ditch it all and go without any religion. Who needs God when you have the Communist Party? However, this is the country that gave the world Mother Theresa; Gjergj Kastrioti (aka Skanderbeg), who fought in defense of Christianity; prominent bishops and imams; even two popes were of Albanian blood. Albania is also the country for the headquarters of a branch of Islam called Bektashi. Today, Albania has three major religions: Roman Catholic, Greek Orthodox, and Islam. Before any of these existed, Albanians were all Pagans. They had their own gods and beliefs until they fell under Roman rule, where they adapted Roman gods, but never fully surrendered their own gods. When the Roman Empire converted to Christianity in 325 AD, Albania, as part of the empire, became Christian too. Not without a fight though. It is said that the people were crucified all over for resisting conversion into Christianity. After the split of Roman Empire to East and West, Albania geographically fell under the Eastern Empire (Byzantine) and thus Christian orthodoxy was imported in some parts closer to Greece, thus close to Constantinople, which is the center of the Orthodox Church. In the fifteenth century, the Ottoman Empire attacked Constantinople and ended the Byzantine Empire and established an empire driven by Islamic law—and thus the Ottoman Empire was born. The Ottoman Empire soon expanded its reach by occupying parts of the Middle East, the Mediterranean, and the Balkan peninsula. Their capital of the empire became Constantinople, which was renamed to Istanbul. Ottomans converted large number of people in the occupied territories to Islam. Albania was not immune to it either, so we now have the third religion, Islam. Real numbers are unknown, but by some accounts about sixty percent of the population is Muslim and the rest is split between Roman Catholic, mainly in the northern parts of the country, and Greek Orthodox in the southern part of the country. Paganism, though gone for close to two thousand years, is still present in many aspects of life in Albania and even some rituals have been blended with Christian or Muslim rituals. For instance, we celebrate many Christian holidays by offering a sacrifice, a lamb usually. It is completely against Catholicism to sacrifice animals, but no one cares. It would in fact be a mortal sin since this would constitute worshipping a Pagan god: direct violation of the first commandments of god that states "You shall have no other gods before me". This is how we have always done it and that's the end of it. Saint Nicholas, the most revered saint in Albania, is celebrated by a sacrifice by almost every Catholic and many Muslims too. You can call this a type of Albanian religion in some aspects.

Historically, the Albanian clergy had been at the forefront of Albanian resistance and had fought for the preservation of culture, language, and sovereignty from other countries that have tried to eliminate it from the map. Members of the catholic clergy, were all from an educated class with degrees from Western universities. Apart from spiritual services, Albanian monasteries also served as preservationists and promoters of Albanian culture, history, and the furtherance of the Albanian cause in the international arena. They were, thus, dangerous to the new communist rulers.

Communists wasted no time in declaring war on religion. First, they attempted to make it unpopular through a propaganda machine designed to discredit any and all members of clergy. When this failed to produce any success, they raised the bar and started imprisoning clergy members. Their charges included anything the Catholic Church was ever accused of as if they were the Vatican elite, or even the pope. Charges included killing Joan of the Arc and Giordano Bruno,[25] leading the various Crusades,[26] and then some more realistic ones, such as allegiance to the Catholic Church's propaganda against Communism and even in some cases where nothing worked, they hid weapons in churches and then accused them of organizing armed uprisings. Why would someone, such as those who were in the Albanian Communist Party who claimed to be the party of the Albanian people, persecute those who had dedicated their lives to preserve and promote the Albanian cause? One reason only: they were not Albanians. Yes, they had Albanian blood in their veins, but that blood was poisoned by Bolshevik ideas and for them ideology—which gave them power—was more important than country. The priority of communists was clear. The city of Shkodër had more prisons than hospitals and possibly even schools. There were twenty-two[27] prisons to be exact, from old dungeons left behind from the Ottoman empire to Gestapo jails. And since these were not enough, they added more by repurposing large houses (after confiscating them from wealthy merchants). They even turned the Franciscan monastery into a jail. How nice of them to keep

---

[25] Joan of Arc was executed for heresy in France, in 1456 and Giordano Bruno was executed in Italy for heresy in 1593.

[26] Crusades were a series of religious wars that took place between tenth and twelfth centuries.

[27] According to Friar Zef Pllumi on his memoir, *Live to Tell*.

the priests jailed in the monastery that was now repurposed to give them a feeling of being at home.

The trials against the clergy were conducted by military tribunals and in some cases the prosecutors and even judges were uneducated people. The trials had become a sad circus where the highly intellectual and educated priests made fun of their persecutors. The prosecutors' questions had answers that were so fine and full of philosophical references that the prosecutors and the judges didn't know how to react. For the fear of being made fun of, they would shut the accused and move on to the next question and then next accused individual. When the circus was too much to bear, the court would adjourn and continue the next day. The next day it would be the same thing all over again, but this time the answers were filled with even more sarcasm and finesse.

Eventually, in 1968, Albania was officially declared an atheist country. At this point, every ordained priest was imprisoned. All their families were sent to suffer harsh conditions in internment camps and harsh persecution was bestowed upon them. No one made it out alive from those prisons until 1990 when all political prisoners were freed under pressure from the West. Almost all the churches and mosques were destroyed. The few that were spared were repurposed, such as the one in my hometown that became a body shop to fix Kooperativë tractors. Crosses were removed from cemeteries. Any religious symbol was eliminated from everywhere and the possession of them meant jail. Even the figure of Gjergj Fishta, a Franciscan bishop and one of the founders of the Albanian alphabet, a great Albanian writer, and a Nobel Prize Literature candidate, was vilified after death (he had died in 1940). His grave was desecrated and his remains were dumped into the river.

In 2018, Pope Francis granted martyrdom to thirty-eight people in Albania and cleared their path to sainthood. The majority of them were priests and some civilian activists who fought for the preservation of Catholic Church and were murdered by communists.

Between 1968 and 1990 many people were imprisoned for things like owing a Bible or reciting a prayer. The enunciation of the word "God" could hand you a sentence of twenty-five years in prison. Prisons were full of political prisoners for crimes committed or made up. People were jailed for things like, "I don't like the bread" to "I pray God…." You didn't even have to say anything to go to jail. You could end up behind bars if someone disliked you and then gave false testimony. People were targeted by the regime and crimes were made up to justify the arrest. Of course, there also were a lot of people who did really break the communist laws and tried to overthrow the regime. They were the real heroes. Political prisoners were a mixture of brave, courageous people who sacrificed everything for the liberation or Albania from communist rule, and a large number of victims were imprisoned because they said something innocent or someone made up a story. Heroes and victims were all one in these confined spaces when they were imprisoned, but they all become heroes in the end. They bounded and resisted and persevered harsh conditions, tortures, and humiliations, but they eventually became winners. Most died waiting for that day.

Now it is all over and religion is free to practice. I don't think there was a law yet to allow it, but simply the mere fact that the priests were out of prison meant it was okay. One day, we got news that a priest who was freed from jail, a sworn anticommunist named Simon Jubani, was going to celebrate a mass by the local cemetery. There were no churches. Cemeteries are considered sacred lands, so the local cemetery was chosen for this first in my lifetime mass celebration. Also, I don't think there would be any church capable of holding the number of people who would participate in that mass. I was fourteen. I had never attended a mass. I was told a little bit about masses by my parents, but couldn't ever imagine what it was like. We did say prayers in secrecy, but that was as much as we could do. From time to time, we had seen a mass on Italian television stations, but that *didn't* really give me the full understanding of it. That in itself—watch a mass on television—was dangerous, but we did it and hoped we would not be caught by the ever-watching eye of secret police. For most major holidays, people were called to some events or activities to distract them and not be able to celebrate any religious holidays. The Christmas tree survived somehow, but was named the New Year tree. Even today, many people call it the New Year tree. Old habits die hard. Santa Claus was called the New Year's grandfather. Growing up, I don't think I knew that they were something else completely. Suffice to say, some of these traditions were more Western Christian traditions and have not been popular in Albania even before the ban of religion. Nowadays, they are as popular as anywhere else.

The day of the mass came. It was a Sunday, as it is customary for Catholics. Everyone—children, men, women, old, young—showed up. Non-Catholics came too. Jesus would be so jealous to see so many people gathered here today that the crowds in Bethlehem must have been much smaller compared to this crowd. I don't think Jesus had ever expected such a turnover at any events celebrating his life. He would be proud too, for this crowd was there in his name. We were there for something else, though, using Jesus as an excuse. We were there to be part of something that was taken away and forbidden for many years.

We were there because now we could. Yes, we were there to attend a Christian mass, but that was not a pure religious pilgrimage, but a celebration of the fall of Communism and the dominance of good versus evil. Jesus or not, this was a good day for us all. The mass was in Latin as it had been the norm before 1968, even though the rules had changed since and now the mass is in local languages. We had no idea what any of those words meant, but were mesmerized. I don't think I had ever heard any Latin word before in my life, but it sounded poetic and divine. We felt drawn back to Jerusalem in the times of Jesus when he was preaching to the Jewish fishermen. The only people who felt somewhat familiar with the practice were older people who remembered mass back in the days. They could cite most of the prayers in Latin phonetically without any knowledge of their meaning. They seemed happy and genuinely close to God. This day is a day I would never forget.

Anyone born after 1968 was not baptized. Anyone married during this time, was not legally married per Church's requirements. All sacraments were missed and people were in disarray with the religious life. Everyone wanted to catch up, but how? The rule is that if you want to baptize your kids, parents need to be baptized and married before God by a priest. How about those couples who missed one or both sacraments because of the twenty-two-year-old ban? No one knew what to do. The priests had no guidance from anyone. No connection with Vatican was established yet, so there was no place to go to get any support. It was similar to the early days of Christianity before the council of Nicaea where no central authority existed. This was an unprecedented case too, so I am not sure if the pope knew what to do either. These people weren't sinners and they had broken no Christian doctrines or tenets; they were simply oblivious of anything and everything religion. These poor priests started with the easy cases: young unbaptized people. I was one of them and so were my three siblings; two brothers and one sister. With a bunch of other kids from the neighborhood we all gathered into a house near ours where a priest baptized us all at once. No godfather was needed, as we were old enough to speak for ourselves now. This amounted to another first: a baptism without a godfather. The purpose of the godfather during baptism is to speak on the child's behalf and accept Christ. We were old and very eager to accept Christ and we could speak for ourselves, or so the priest said. We had done it long time ago. No matter how much communists tried to make us forget him, the closer we grew to Jesus. Eventually, they figured out a solution and the pope issued a decree, a type of amnesty, where everyone in Albania who had missed the sacraments because of the religion ban were pardoned and the sacraments were bestowed to them all by special decree. My baptism, like most events of my early life, was anything but ordinary.

IV.   Why Don't You Just Stay Dead

They say a cat has nine lives. Cats barely get injured whereas dogs do get injured easily. Communism must have had ten or twenty lives because it survived wave after wave of protests and demonstrations and even after the first so-called free elections. Communism must be a special cat breed. After many rallies and uninterrupted unrest in Albania, the communist government finally agreed to the formation of other political parties, which were illegal until then. It was a case of going from one-party rule to pluralism.

The first opposition party created was the Democratic Party, which is the rightwing party, followed by the Republican Party. Many other political parties sprung like mushrooms soon that we lost count of them. The one that mattered, though, was the Democratic Party. This was the first, well-established party and people quickly rallied behind it. We needed something to lean on and had found it. As per politics or programs or other stuff that mattered, we knew little. There was only one party until then, the self-proclaimed "Nëna Parti," the mother party. We knew even less of people within this new party. It would come as a big surprise to many later on to find out that the leader of this Party, Sali Berisha, was himself a communist and a physician of Hoxha. But that was a little secret we were willing to ignore. At the same time, the communist party (which was called "People's Party" at this time) led by the ruthless dictator Ramiz Alia, was renamed to the Socialist Party as a way to distance itself from the past; Mr. Alia appointed himself the President of Albania. Communist dictators never used this title, as it was deemed capitalistic in nature. The first elections were held on March 31, 1991. People were eager to vote and most importantly to cast their vote against the Socialist Party. As we were all waiting for the announcement of the results, to our great surprise and disappointment, the Socialist Party was declared the winner—and by a landslide no less. *How could this be*, everyone thought? The elections were clearly and unequivocally manipulated and stolen and people were not having it. No one in their right mind believed this to be the will of the people. Demonstrations erupted again and this time with more fury. Several people were killed from sniper fire and their killers have yet to face the justice. Most notably, in Shkodër, three prominent Democratic leaders were shot dead in broad daylight at a peaceful demonstration. This happened on April 2, 1991, and it is remembered throughout Albania as the "Protestat e dy Prillit" (the April 2[n] Protests). No matter how much we tried, this regime just wouldn't die. How many lives does this cat breed have? How many more lives would it claim before taking its last breath? The country was exhausted from a long dictatorship, a bloody transition period, and fraudulent elections, elections that were so anticipated across the country.

Demonstrations didn't cease until the government was forced to accept the creation of a provisory government and set a date for new elections. A new government with participation from all parties was assembled under Prime Minister Ylli Bufi and a second election was held on March 22, 1992. No one knew Mr. Bufi before and he never made it to the spotlight after. He was a ghost. God knows where he came from, but we needed a non-controversial figure for at least several months to lead the country and to get the bloodshed to stop. He did all right under the circumstances. Election campaigns took over the country and while sympathizers of one party were having a rally, the adversaries would interrupt and brawls would break out all over the country. Many people were hurt and died. Party leaders continued with their rhetoric and crowds cheered until their teeth were about to fall off.

A second election was held under tense circumstances and was closely watched by international observers from any agency you can think of such as UN, UE, OSBE, and all other acronyms. People on both sides kept a close eye on things to make sure the opposing side wasn't stealing their votes. It was impossible for the observers to cover every election poll, and given the manual process it wasn't that hard to escape their wandering eyes. What worked best was the fact that Democratic Party was better organized now and had many volunteers to ensure integrity at the polls. The night the election results were announced, which took several days after the elections, was a moment of solace. Joyous people ran through streets and squares to celebrate. Albanian and American flags covered the horizon near and far. Cheers and songs erupted. The Democratic Party of Albania had won the elections by a landslide. The snake's head was finally cut off. The cat ran out of lives. Albania was free. We all wondered now if this beast would stay dead for good.

My family had been a strong opponent of the regime throughout its existence and had paid a heavy price for it. We were outcasts, shamed, and shunned from the community. We had been put in a ghetto but without the Star of David on our arms. Everyone had known who were and there was no place to hide. We had been labeled as people who don't belong in society. "Enemies of the people" and other names and labels had been thrown at us. Bottom line, we were different and did not deserve the same rights as other people. Our only choice was to cope with this. What other choice did we have? I had hard time grasping this situation, and for a long time I didn't want to believe it, but then it became a part of my identity so much so that I even embraced it. My parents tried hard to explain without making me upset. They tried to explain it more like a fate, or an honor to be with this undeterred, anti-terror class. Government had no problem calling us undeserved names, but our parents couldn't even explain to us kids why we weren't able to go on a field trip with other kids. How far could evil really go? There was no end to it. Now when you think of how very few rights anyone had in that extreme form of Communism, and thinking of someone having even less, you know that we had nothing: no control of any aspects of our lives. Period. For forty-eight years the communist government had been controlling us day and night, but now, it was over. Now we could say out loud without fear of persecution, "No more!"

We finally woke up from a terrible dream. We couldn't believe it, but it was true.

V.   Free at last

With freedom, came confusion and corruption, among other things. We began to see the world and wanted to be like other people. We wanted to be part of the developed world—and quickly. Waves of migration swept up people of all ages. Everyone wanted to flee the country in pursuit of a better life. People crossed borders to reach Yugoslavia and Greece, and sailed to Italy, by all means of transportation, from small fishing boats to hiding inside cargo ships as well as the infamous "gomone," rubber speed boats that were meant for fishing and pleasure trips. These were overloaded with forty to fifty people and crossed the Adriatic to Italy. Smuggling became a lucrative business in the coastal city of Vlore, while several people drowned and died in search of a better life. Migration became an obsession. It became a stage of life everyone had to go through. It became like a pillar of a religion, something everyone must follow. Of course, these events didn't pass without their effects on our family either. Apart from my two brothers who had escaped, all my siblings, after the fall of Communism, migrated to Italy during the next ten years. Some made a life there and some left for greener pastures. My brother, Rrok, and I came to America and joined Marash, where we made a home with no plans to go anywhere else. The day I became American citizen, March 31, 2010, was one of the happiest days of my life. The

American dream for many means owning a home and having a good job. For me the American dream became a reality the day I set foot on this blessed soil. I realized it the day I could say "God Bless America" without fear of someone hearing me and sending me jail. The rest is a bonus.

In 1994, as soon as I turned seventeen, I enlisted in Albania's mandatory military service. Nothing had changed in terms of how the country maintained its military from the Communist era. Every male citizen had to serve, unless there were some special circumstances that prevented you from enrolling. I could have postponed it for a year or two, but decided to go. The previous regime deprived my family from just about anything, but the new democratic government tried to be conscious about it and tried to compensate the Të Prekun in some way. The label was now changed from Të Prekun to "Ish të Përndjekurit Politikë" (ex-politically prosecuted). While Të Prekun came with harsh consequences, Ish të Përndjekurit Politikë came with benefits. I was assigned to the navy and appointed to serve in a submarine in the biggest naval base in South Albania. While my older brothers who served during Communism weren't permitted to hold a real gun (wooden guns were given instead), I was given a rank that was equivalent to a petty officer. I proudly wore the navy uniform and my rank. For the first time in my short life I felt I belonged in this country, and felt proud and ready to defend it. Boy! I felt good!

Military service wasn't bad. I matured and learned a few things. I learned how to be independent. I learned teamwork. I became a man, as they say. After completing my fifteen months of mandatory service, I was discharged and went back home to a civilian life. Here I was: just over eighteen years of age, with lots of dreams and no experience of anything useful. We had the land and the livestock now. We grew just about everything from vegetables to corn and raised livestock. I became a farmer, you could say. I was free and happy. We made enough food to feed the family and had plenty of time in our hands. Life started to make sense for my parents who lived most of their lives under oppression. As for me, I didn't know any better. All this was new to me. My whole life had been under the regime and I didn't know that a different life was possible, a life that was different from ours, a life where you can decide for yourself. Freedom!

I hear a lot people in America or other Western countries express disbelief when people in oppressed countries appear to embrace the regime. In some cases, I've heard people quote blogs and then consider any information they would find there as the "voice of the people." These people—Americans and other Europeans—don't know the degree to which oppressed people across the globe are deprived of the ability to think and talk. It was like everyone was performing a script written by the government. Unless you have lived in a country like Communist Albania, you may never fully understand what people went through. As the expression goes, you have no idea. Life in a totalitarian regime is a whole 'nother ball game. I lived my first fourteen years of my life within one—and it was long enough to make me hate it with my whole being.

5. Heroes and Victims

We often confuse heroes with victims. While no one succeeded in overthrowing the regime, many tried. Blood was shed and lives were lost. These were the real heroes. As for our family and others like us, we were victims because we had some heroes. I applaud them for doing what they did to oppose the regime, some with sweat and tears, and others with their lives. These heroes are to be applauded for trying to get us to see and have a better life, and for many, a life that nobody ever imagined. Me, I was sentenced before I was born. I was guilty at birth for a crime I never knew I had committed. I was a victim.

You should never have to thank someone for doing the right thing. But if you live in a world where doing the right thing is hard to do, then doing the right thing can be considered heroism. In the Communist regime, the rules had changed. Doing the right thing no longer meant helping an elderly person cross the street. Doing the right thing meant putting your life in danger for someone else. The ones who chose to do the right thing were heroes too. No question about it. But that doesn't mean we can blame people for not mustering the courage to be heroes. We can only blame the regime who gave people a difficult choice to make. Not everyone can be a hero.

There were other heroes as well and these were in the lines of communists. I'm speaking of those who objected to partaking in atrocities. These people, of course, had to pay with their lives for opposing the regime. The people who supported and helped others throughout the years, all the while putting their own lives and families at risk, were heroes. Whether it was the minister refusing to sign a death sentence, a judge refusing to send an innocent person to jail, the young officer who saved my father's life, or a local leader who wrote a good reference letter for an anti-communist, they were all heroes. There were good-hearted people who had become communists to survive but had nothing in common with the oppressors. They were sheep in wolves clothing. They have my admiration and eternal gratitude.

6. No One is Without Sin

In the Christian Bible there is a story of Jesus sitting and writing on the ground with a stick when along came a mob of mad people chasing a woman named Mary Magdalene. They were holding rocks and shouting at her. When the mob arrived, Jesus asked them why they wanted to stone the woman. They said that she had committed adultery. Jesus said, *"Let him who is without sin cast the first stone!"* One after the other all of them dropped their stones and left.

I have been asked many times by non-Albanians and Albanians from a younger generation, *"Why was this allowed to go on for so long?"* Another fact, apart from the ones I've already discussed, is that the communists succeeded in getting people to turn against each other. Divide and conquer. The regime had been successful in making every person become part of a machine that was designed to serve the regime. Every one played a role, big or some small. In some cases, a contribution was given without knowledge. It all worked like a well-oiled machine.

There was one police officer in charge of about 13,000 people in our municipality, for instance; he managed just fine without having to lift a finger. If he wanted someone arrested, he didn't bother to go get them. Instead, he summoned them to show up at his office. No one dared disobey such a request. When he walked in the streets, everyone went into hiding. You didn't do anything wrong, but it didn't matter. Everyone was afraid they would be next. If you saw a cop walking toward you, you turned the other way. It's just the way it was. Cops where never there to assist anyone; they were there to get someone. Calling police for help? You only called to rat out someone. Some of the things that qualified as do's and don'ts were incredible. For example, a "wrong" laugh or laughing at the wrong person, or not laughing at a joke said by someone of high rank could get you in trouble. And if an offense wasn't on the list, it could be added. That's how it went: sentence first, then find the crime to fit the sentence.

This was survival of the fittest at its best: even to the extent that a brother would turn against a brother. There are many cases where one brother was a die-hard communist and another a political prisoner. One was a war martyr and another was shot and killed without any due process. People were encouraged to spy and tell on every move. There was almost no one you could trust, not even your own shadow. The brutality of Communism had no boundaries. Some people reported on others for favors, some for fear, and some for pure sadistic pleasure. Other people would spy and make false allegations if they didn't like you. Turning people against each other was a low-cost effective method for the regime. If we had been more united, the regime might've fallen a lot sooner, but the regime's brutality had the population living in a state of constant fear and afraid for our own lives. And then we began to rise up.

As for the regime's demise, it can be easily argued that the regime had no one else to blame but itself: keeping everyone in a population on a short leash would eventually and inevitably lead to an uprising. The desire for freedom can never be squelched or stamped out. And yet the regime ruled for as long as it did because it forced everyone to play their part—to behave—or else face an awful punishment or death. Communism ruled Albania for forty-eight years with an iron fist and was finally defeated in March 31, 1992, but it will take decades more to repair the widespread damage caused by the regime. The fabric of society was torn, and it will take a long time to sew it up.

This is a small window into my life growing up in communist Albania. My story is not an isolated case, but one of many throughout the country. Historians will find an epidemic of cases out there. I hope they are eventually revealed because tales like these need to be heard by everyone.

Made in United States
North Haven, CT
20 December 2024

63153667R00143